Ammo Grrrll Aims True

By Susan Vass

Volume 2   2015-16

Copyright © 2015-18 Susan Vass
All Rights Reserved

ISBN: 978-1-7327370-5-1

All rights are reserved under International and Pan-American copyright conventions. Without written permission of the author no part of this book may be reproduced, transmitted, or down-loaded by any means electronic or mechanical, including but not limited to photocopying, recording, down-loading, or reverse engineering, nor may it be stored or otherwise introduced into any information storage and retrieval system by any means now known or hereafter invented.

Also by Susan Vass:
   Ammo Grrrll Hits The Target (Volume 1; 2014-15)

Also published by VWAM, LLC:
   Khaybar, Minnesota, by Max Cossack

DEDICATION

To my dear parents with great love and profound gratitude. To my mother, Dorothy Terry Baumbach, of blessed memory, and my father, James Baumbach, still soldiering on at Edgewood Vista Assisted Living, thanks to the loving and excellent staff of caregivers there.

Whatever that saying is about giving a child roots to be grounded and wings to fly applies to my parents in spades. I never play the Lottery because I figure I have already won.

One of the first crop of Baby Boomers, I was blessed to be raised in a small town in the American Heartland in a tiny historical window of peace, prosperity, and two-parent families. Though eventually five of us shared about 1500 square feet, one bathroom, one black wall telephone, one car, and one television that got one channel – all unthinkable hardships in today's modern families -- we were solid middle-middle class. Almost everybody was, in fact. It was a great time to be a kid.

WHEREIN AMMO GRRRLL INTRODUCES HERSELF

First of all, thank you for buying this book. This is Volume 2 of what will eventually be at least a five-volume set, perhaps more than that and stretching into Infinity, like the number of times I have lost the same ten pounds.

I am a regular Friday columnist for a popular on-line center-right site called Power Line. This book, and the previous one, called *Ammo Grrrll Hits The Target, Volume 1* for your convenience, are compilations of a year's worth of those columns, plus a few bonus pages, for explanation, or let's face it, just plain filler material.

I am a small but sturdy woman of late, late middle age, residing in the great state of Arizona in a Dusty Little Village. After retiring from some 30 years as a standup comic, I moved here from Minnesota with my husband, the famous novelist, Max Cossack. In 2012 we took up target shooting at the exact moment in time – how very like me! -- that ammo became very scarce. This required standing in long Soviet-style lines – at Walmart, at Cabelas, at wherever ammo might be sold. I acquired the nickname of Ammo Grrrll from my fellow line-standers and also the many clerks who got to know us by the hours we spent standing around.

In March of 2014, I organized my "Thoughts from the Ammo Line" into a column and submitted it on spec to a friendly acquaintance of mine, Scott Johnson, who was one of four brilliant political writers at Power Line. He liked it, posted it, and I have been writing for them ever since. It is a great honor and privilege to have such a platform to make whatever small contribution I can make to both conservative thought and stress-relieving humor.

Volume 1 was organized by categories, but Volume 2 presents the columns in the order in which they appeared that year. Who knows how Volume 3 will be organized? Perhaps as an anagram from the first letter of each column. I can be a whimsical gal at times.

MORE HONORABLE MENTIONS

I don't know how many of my readers – especially those who just picked this book at random off Amazon – know about how BlogWorld works. There are sites and they contain articles; people comment on the articles. Then people comment on the comments. Even though many use pen names and "handles", others get to know who they are by their styles and viewpoints. Most of it is very democratic and convivial. The Ace of Spades site, for example, even maintains a Prayer List.

Sometimes, nasty people weigh in with such witty and perceptive comments as "You suck. You are a stupid Nazi f*head who sucks. I hate you and all your racist friends and you all suck." These people are called "trolls". It is my understanding that some of them are even paid, although it has been my experience in this life that there are certified lunatics aplenty who are often real self-starters even without remuneration. If the trolls are obnoxious or obscene enough, eventually they will be banned, especially on the site for which I write, Power Line.

Since I don't even maintain a Facebook page, I often treat my column and its commenters as a kind of on-line family, sharing good news and bad, inquiring about the goings-on of other commenters.

In Volume 1, I singled out a whole group of Top Commenters for a group mention and then highlighted one particular fellow who had commented favorably on every single dang column in almost five years.

I jokingly said that the others could compete for Most Obsequious and get plucked out for an Honorable Mention in subsequent volumes. But it's a real problem for me. Mr. Davis was the undisputed King, but after that, there are literally DOZENS of smart, witty and consistent commenters.

So, in Volume 2 I am going to channel Willie and Julio and salute "To All the Girls I've LIKED Before". These ladies – and many others! – comment on a very regular basis and I often hit the little up arrow to "like" what they have contributed. They are Deb from Montana; Tracy from Elk River, MN; Abby from Florida; Heather, from the great state of Texas, and Ladyhawk from Alexandria, MN. And yes, Ladyhawk is her given name. Just as my given name is "Ammo". Haha. I kid. Before Power Line switched to Disqus from Facebook, there were also Mary Louise, Dorothy, Olyvia and Colleen.

For the rest of you, I hope this kind of "inside baseball" little shout-out hasn't been off-putting. Please visit Power Line on a regular basis, if you're not already a regular, and by Volume 3, "Ammo Grrrll Returns Fire", you will be familiar with our very large cast of characters.

A Footnote: Oh, and TonyP wanted to be a Footnote. Consider it done, TonyP. And thank you for your terrific posts and your service.

THE CONTEXT

Volume 2 runs from April 3, 2015 to April 1, 2016

Volume 2's columns appear at a rather "yuge" historic moment, both politically and personally for me. For Volume 2 covers the run-up to the 2016 election with all its drama, shock, awe, and what seemed like hundreds of Republican contenders, including a bizarre outsider named Donald John Trump.

Don't worry. He has no chance. Everybody who's anybody says so. To this day you can YouTube "people who said Trump would NEVER be President" and be entertained for many minutes by dozens of celebrities, unbiased news readers, elected officials, and assorted pontificating authorities who are much smarter than the rest of us. Experts, one and all.

The historic 2016 election itself will not be until Volume 3.

By the end of the 2015-16 "Ammo Grrrll Year" which runs from March to March, I will also have lost my beloved mother. I was one of the last people in my high school class to still have both of my parents alive and of sound mind. Though I never took that for granted, on some level I guess, I thought that would last forever. But nothing does.

We need to take a page from Robin Williams' great turn in *Dead Poets' Society* and *carpe diem,* seize the day, every day. If you still are blessed to have parents, give them a call. Send a card. Hug your kids. And then, lock them out in the yard – your parents or your kids, whatever -- and sit down in a comfortable chair with good lighting, a beverage or two, perhaps a nice snack on the end table (Nachos, cupcakes, a bag of popcorn, some Cheetos) and start this book. Don't forget to have Wet Wipes handy as

Cheetos can be messy and will turn your pages orange. Orange pages bad.

With only so much time left, if you only read one book of political humor columns, make it this one. You won't be sorry.

APRIL, MAY, AND JUNE, 2015

Once, long long ago in San Francisco, Mr. Ammo Grrrll and I both took karate. One of the competing dojos (studios) in the same Chinese style (Kenpo), featured an owner/instructor who had three daughters, named April, May, and June.

That has absolutely nothing further to do with any of my columns, but seeing those months as a heading reminded me of that memory. And also of sitting for twelve hours on backless high school gym bleachers for a karate tournament in which Mr. AG competed. I was about 57 months pregnant at the time and weighed just under a thousand pounds, and that was just the water retention in my ankles. Now that I think about it, it may have only been in my 9th month. That baby is now 45 at this writing.

Funny what will trigger a memory. Anyway, back to a brief guide for what to expect in Volume 2 of the Ammo Grrrll series.

We begin the second Ammo Grrrll Year with a pleasant gathering on our patio, a practice Mr. Ammo Grrrll dubbed "Gracious Living".

Might as well rest up because we are about to go on a long 6-part journey together from Arizona to Minnesota and back that will take us all the way to mid-May.

In May, you will find two of my personal favorites when I take on some politically-correct cultural lunacy about the unfair advantage of reading to one's children, and a second column that will recall those halcyon days in San Francisco when feminist extremism was just getting a real talon-hold on the culture.

And, just like that, we are already to summer!

June's columns include suggestions for campaign slogans for some of the many contenders in the upcoming 2016 election, my take on the "Mattress Girl" college "rape" controversy, my annual Father's Day tribute, and ends with "Yes Means Yes" and what the new step-by-step permission to proceed romantically will mean for sex, literature and even for porn. Fasten your seatbelts, friends; it's gonna be a bumpy ride.

Gracious Living

April 3, 2015

When we moved from our winter rental in Palm Springs to our new home in Arizona in 2010, we were invited on our very first night to a little get-together of Minnesota snowbirds at the home of John and Angela, long-time friends from back home.

This was a welcome relief as we were basically "camping out" in our new home. Our furniture would not arrive for a week, so John and Angela gave us two plastic patio chairs, and a 12-inch television. We purchased a card table with four chairs that clearly had won a design contest for "most hideously uncomfortable chair ever". Probably created by a chiropractor hoping for future business. To eat a brief meal was to risk permanent paralysis.

We had arranged to spend the nights in a hotel some 20 miles away. Our Dusty Little Village has only a "virtual" hotel, which is to say, a hotel that has been promised for about seven years. It has yet to appear but surely will at the same time Obamacare "bends the cost curve."

Minnesotans are notoriously thrifty and the new couple we had just met – Don and Margie – were grievously offended by the thought of our spending six nights in a hotel waiting for our bed to appear. They offered an inflatable queen-sized bed which turned out to be surprisingly adequate. I worried the whole first night about scorpions being able to get on a foot-high bed. Later, of course, I learned that scorpions can get anywhere, including but not limited to, the bathroom vanity drawer. Scorpion in your hairbrush? Surprise!! So you either have to worry all the time or not at all. I'll take "not at all" for $300, Alex. So far, my Scorpion Score is Ammo Grrrll: 8; Scorpions: Zero. (Stomped, not shot.

The HOA and local constabulary frown on gunfire within a dwelling. Plus one word: ricochet.)

Back to the welcoming get-together: It was late January; the patio screen doors were open and people were walking in shirtsleeves on the trail down the greenbelt between the back yards. Let me repeat, Rust Belt denizens: JANUARY! A lazy ceiling fan was turning, and, inspired by good bourbon and good company, Mr. Ammo Grrrll exulted, "Boy, this is really Gracious Living! I've only seen gatherings this gracious in fancy magazines!"

And so began a tradition, soon shortened to GL.

It takes remarkably little to have a wonderful time. People squander fortunes on expensive "toys," elaborate vacations, pathetic status symbols. When we send out the emails to gather for GL, we are looking at some thrown-together cheese and crackers (cheese and matzo this week), chips and dips, and drinks on the patio with fun, funny, easy-going people. Before you can say "flash mob", the emails have done their job and the Geezer-Americans begin to walk and bike toward the designated patio. Dress ranges from jeans and gun-themed t-shirts to shorts and sports-themed t-shirts. Except for Mr. Ammo Grrrll, dapper in his Dress Black Sweatpants. We have all lived far too long to try to impress each other. Which is too bad in a way because many people would have impressive tales if they felt like bragging.

We catch each other up on good news and sad; on grandchildren and elder care. Those that still have them talk about their jobs; those without them discuss golf scores, a paddle and net game called pickleball that swept the Sun Belt a few years ago, politics, and cholesterol tests; we help each other try to remember the titles of movies we have seen as recently as the day before yesterday. ("You know that one about the Seals with the guy who was also in a boy band?") We recommend TV series we have enjoyed on Netflix. *Justified*, *Longmire*, *Lilyhammer*, *Game of Thrones*, and *Breaking Bad* are particular favorites among our friends, though I personally have not seen the latter two.

In many ways, the late 50s, 60s, 70s remind me of being a kid. Remember how easy it was to make a friend when you were a kid? Basically, a kid showed up, started kicking a can around in your presence or throwing a ball in the air, and before you knew it, you were playing together. Stand around with a bottle of beer near Gracious Living, and you will be invited in.

Ammo Grrrll, are you saying this is The Dawning of the Age of Aquarius? Sadly, no. You still have your jerks who believe the HOA rules are Holy Writ: "And God spake to the Hebrews and the mixed multitude as well and said, 'there shalt be only this type of chicken wire around the plants that the bunnies eat, and not the other type of wire. I know not why, but I have spake. Also, no little wooden burros except in the back. Orange ceramic pigs – fair enough; but little wooden burros shalt thee not have, nay not one.'" The HOA tattlers are the same people who were room monitors when Teacher left the room. I loathed tattlers as a kid, and still do.

But they are easily avoided. So, young people, fear not your senior years. As the late, great Will Rogers said, "One of the many things no one tells you about aging is that it is such a nice change from being young." On this first night of Passover, may we all have a year of good health and Gracious Living. Next year in Jerusalem. And A Very Happy Easter to our Christian readers and friends.

VISITING MY PEOPLE 1

April 10, 2015

My parents were celebrating their 70th wedding anniversary (Holy Moly, Rocky!), followed four days later, by my Mother's 94th birthday. (More on these in Part Six. Hang in there with me!) It was time to leave Arizona for Minnesota. In March, the iffiest of months, weather-wise.

We have discussed my aversion to flying. And this was before an insane co-pilot locked the pilot out and dive-bombed into the Swiss Alps. I prefer to stay on the ground. But even more than the fear of flying is my absolute love affair with this country, which you cannot see from 30,000 feet any more than you can get to know a person from across the room.

Cities are fine and I have lived in or near them for much of my life. But it's small-town heartland that I love the most. These are – as our Attorney General said – "my people." Now, sadly, Mr. Holder was simply talking about people the same color as he, a shameful and racist thing for someone charged with upholding "blind" justice to say, even if he thought it.

So, early on a Sunday morning, off I went.

Before we begin: A tutorial on Passing. People, people, people! When you are fixin' to pass, here's what you do: put on your blinker, move briskly into the left-hand lane, and then use your accelerator (hint: it's the one on the right…) to actually get PAST the car or truck and back into the right-hand lane. Hence, the name: passing. If you just pull parallel with the vehicle you are intending to pass and stay there for many, many miles, you have failed to execute the most important part of "passing." You are not passing, you are annoying. The song notwithstanding, YOU may "love a parade," but not everyone else shares your delight, particularly when 40 cars are tailgating at 80 mph waiting for you to pass.

One of the first things you learn when you spend time among actual "facts on the ground," is that virtually everything the liberals say is a lie. Everything. A couple of examples.

Oh, Lord, can we all become any more nauseated and bored from hearing about our terrible systemic raaacism? I overnighted in Pecos, TX, in what turned out to be a very expensive "budget" motel because the town was filled with oil workers who had taken all the rooms and the hoteliers were gouging like crazy, because, presumably, the oil companies were paying the bills. I went next door to eat supper and at table after table were ethnically-mixed groups of sturdy young roughnecks – white guys, black guys, Mexican guys, Indian guys – all joking and talking, eating enormous quantities and playing with their cellphones, phoning wives, or girlfriends. Where was the terrible "racism" that would prevent these non-whites from being hired in the first place, or prevent friendship groups from forming?

What to make of the two beautiful young Texas women – one black, one white – who just struck up a conversation with my friend and me in downtown Ft. Worth and delighted to hear us speak "Minnesotan" with the long "oh" in Minnesota? Or the Mexican couple from California who just talked and joked around with us at the Rest Area? Most people who are not liberals just see people and don't obsess about race and color. They really don't.

Secondly. If you hear the word "infrastructure," be prepared for a web of lies that ends with somebody's brother-in-law and

Democrat donor getting a big fat contract to do something unnecessary and expensive. I traveled about 4500 miles on highways and byways, and something so small that Garmin just called it "Road," and the much-maligned "infrastructure" in this country is in spectacular shape. The whole highway system is a bloomin' miracle. God Bless Ike. Remember Shecky Obama yukkin' it up over the lack of "shovel-ready" projects? What a card! Every word out of his mouth is shovel-ready.

I do love the fact that Philosophy Majors have been hired – at last! – to write copy for road signs. How else to explain the existential quality of "Dust Storms May Exist." or "Zero Visibility Possible"? "Bridge Ices Before Road" is probably useful information, but at 78 degrees in Oklahoma, I just went ahead and took the chance. "Watch for Falling Rock" is less than helpful without the slightest hint of what to do if, while watching, you spot rock falling. There is no Falling Rock Escape Route. The signs warning people not to pick up hitchhikers because they may be escaped prisoners are also valuable, if somewhat depressing. But any country that needs a sign that says "Do Not Drive Into Smoke" may be doomed.

VISITING MY PEOPLE 2

April 17, 2015

A road trip across this great and beautiful land produces some delightful surprises. Just outside Deming, NM, on farm or ranch land, I saw a large homemade sign, "Stand with Israel." It gladdened my heart for many miles. God Bless You, whoever you are. In West Texas, I regret that I passed up the advertised opportunity to purchase TNT on a 2 for 1 sale. For the 94-year-old mother who has everything. And wants to downsize.

I love Texas, don't get me wrong, and would probably live there if I didn't live in Arizona. But you folks do hit the "Alamo" and "Lone Star" stuff about as hard as Georgians hit "Peachtree."

Texas is big. (No, really, it is). And El Paso is like a microcosm of Texas itself: it takes about 40 minutes to get through it even with decent traffic. It starts with discount furniture places and tire sellers and Gentlemen's Clubs, and goes on and on and on through hundreds of small businesses with Spanish names (and Alamo and Lone Star).

I love all those hard-working entrepreneurial people of every race and color who "didn't build that," according to President Useless Community Organizer. My family owned a drugstore in which my father worked about 100 hours a week. Claiming "he didn't build that" – without even issuing a "trigger warning" – makes me so upset I may need a "safe room" with plush toys in order to recover. And money. I think I need money for that.

Any American President who can say something that stupid and offensive about small business should not get to retire on a massive government pension in a mega-mansion in Hawaii. Or get a $20 million-dollar advance for a post-Presidential book: *Audaciously Bad Things: The Crusades, Israel, and Sand Traps* (Bill Ayers, call your office…) as he waits to become the UN Secretary-General or Twelfth Caliph.

In honor of my own *Dreams From My Father*, I wish there were a way to compel Obama to run a family restaurant for a few years. See how he enjoys dealing with regulatory agencies, the IRS, OSHA, employees who call in sick on Saturday night, and customers who load their plates for the fourth time on the all-you-can-eat lunch buffet and then leave most of it uneaten. There goes your profit margin, but it's OK, because profit is evil, anyway.

Speaking of restaurants, in Sweetwater, Texas, I went looking for what I had been promised by Glenn the Gun Guy, my shooting instructor, was the best food on planet earth. Glenn is not a small man. He knows guns and he knows food. I circled around in downtown Sweetwater for about 20 minutes looking for Miss Allen's Family Style Restaurant until a lovely young woman gave me perfect directions with the admonition "You better be hungry." Alas and alack, it was closed Mondays! Granola bars just didn't cut it after such anticipation.

It goes without saying that there are jackasses everywhere. But, in general, small town America is kind, friendly, and helpful. In the 70s and 80s, many plots for *Mannix* and *Cannon* and like television dramas had the hero's car breaking down in a small town, usually in the South, populated solely by knuckle-dragging cretins who were all related to the corrupt sheriff. Even when we were much less conservative, Mr. Ammo Grrrll and I mocked these shows and said, "I bet whoever wrote this drivel has never been in a town smaller than L.A. in his life."

In Dudley's Corner Cafe in Latimer, Iowa, a sweet couple walked in, looked around at the regulars and then straight at me in my Ruger shirt, and said, "You must be the one with the Arizona plates." There then ensued a lively, cafe-wide discussion of Concealed Carry and Spring Training baseball. They were just back from Mesa themselves.

Earlier, in Missouri, I had noticed that my "low tire pressure" sign had come on. I am about as helpless with car things as I am with computer things. Which is one of the reasons we have men. (There are others.) I went into a travel plaza and asked a Mexican truck driver at the coffee machine if he had a tire gauge. He did not seem to understand the question and was preoccupied with getting coffee. Fair enough. In Spanish I either thanked him or possibly told him that my dog was sick and the sky was blue. It's hard to tell with my Spanish.

I went outside and a nicely-dressed gentleman drove up and parked. He did have a tire gauge, checked all my tires for me in a cold stiff wind, and pronounced me good to go. Just then the Mexican guy came out and had BOUGHT a tire gauge! He wouldn't even let me reimburse him. Guess he felt sorry for me with my sick dog.

Oh, those awful men and their "rape culture." So now I own a tire gauge which is part-way to knowing how to use it to diagnose the problem and then solve it. Or I could just find more random nice men. Yeah, I think I'll go with that.

VISITING MY PEOPLE 3

April 24, 2015

It could have been infinitely worse, of course. My mother reported just this past Tuesday that Minnesota was snowy and bitter cold. So, in mid- to late-March on the way to or from Minnesota, I could have been stranded in an epic blizzard and still be catatonic in the fetal position in a motel in Wichita. "Possibly the fetal position," commented Mr. AG, "but never catatonic." He's getting Liver and Lima Bean Surprise for dinner.

I encountered no blizzards, but still it was not always easy.

First, let's talk about the wind. From West Texas, up Tornado Alley, and into Kansas of Toto and Dorothy fame, to Iowa and northern Minnesota, I never had a day without fierce wind. The kind of gale where it's very difficult to open your car door to fill up at a gas station, until you put your shoulder into it. My wee hands were stiff and sore from clutching the steering wheel to keep the car on the road. What it does for a hairdo shouldn't even be mentioned. Think Margaret Hamilton in the aforementioned Wizard of Oz, only more unkempt.

I never saw the sun for eleven straight days. Then there was rain. As I left Minnesota headed for Des Moines, there was a light drizzle. When I crossed into Iowa, the rain started in earnest and the temperatures continued to drop. 36-35-34-33. I knew from wretched experience what happens to roads once rain turns to freezing rain and sleet. At 32 degrees, I gave up and left the Highway. In Ankeny, Iowa, I got the very last room in a Marriott Courtyard, which happened to be a handicapped-accessible suite priced at $189.00, plus hefty taxation without representation. I took it in gratitude and warmth and waded back out to get my things. What is more comfy than soaking wet tennis shoes? It was the only pair I had packed as I was not in a covered wagon and had not planned on fording any streams.

When leaving Minnesota, I had put my suitcase in the trunk, closed but unzipped, fixin' to put a few souvenirs in it from inside the car. Ah, you fellow short-term-memory-challenged persons know exactly where this is going. I grabbed my suitcase and yanked it out of the trunk. It opened (doh!) and everything flew into the wet parking lot, some items at an impressive distance. This increased my resolve to get more attractive underwear. The 5-Second Rule does not work any better for clothing than it does for dropped candy. You never saw anyone shovel clothes into a suitcase any faster, but still it was severely damp. Blessed is she who can laugh at herself for she will never run out of material. Drenched and laughing hysterically, I'm sure I looked like an escaped lunatic. Not for the first time.

The next day my plan was either to end up in Wichita, if I was tired, or Guthrie, Oklahoma. Why Guthrie, you ask? I was tasked with retrieving the little Nexus with the Candy Crush game I had left in my room on the way up. It is debatable which is more embarrassing: leaving the game (more on lost objects in Part Five) or playing the game for hundreds of misspent hours to just shy of Level 500. At least, I've never given the malevolent geniuses at King Corporation one thin dime. I used to think Sudoku was addictive. That was just the gateway drug to Candy Crush. Which is yet more pointless, if that is possible.

Now, the way I have always gone from Arizona back to Mordor is 10 East to 20/30 East to 35W North. And, obviously, back the same way. I stick like grim death to those trusted highways, especially if I am alone. Even armed, safety trumps reckless adventure.

But I had borrowed The Paranoid Texan's Garmin and he had spent considerable time helping me program it. OK, programming it. And even though Guthrie is a straight shot down 35, Garmin was determined for me to see Joplin, MO and Tulsa before I die. She is one bossy little GPS system. She gets wrapped around the axle when I leave the highway to get gas. ("Re-calculating. Again. Sigh.") I don't know if she thought I would save 3 minutes or what.

I won't soon forget Tulsa. I hit it at rush hour in blinding rain and wind. My windshield wipers could no way keep up. Then came the 2-inch hail. The locusts were scheduled, but were crushed by the hailstones. The last 78 miles to Guthrie, Garmin put me on 33 West, something even she just called a "road", by which she meant a two-lane road with oncoming traffic. Tornadoes were all over the area. Two of my fellow human beings decided that now would be a good time to take their pre-fab homes out for a spin on a flat-bed truck. But it was all perfectly safe what with the "Wide Load" signs on them. At one point we also stopped dead for 20 minutes for some kind of road repair which had turned the two-lane road into a one-lane trail. The poor men standing out there in the hail and the rain had to make us take turns.

And you know what? It was some of the most beautiful country I've ever been through. Huge rolling hills, so steep and frequent they reminded me of that old ribbon Christmas candy, all green and spring-like, with one small town after another with great names like Drumright and Cushing, and speed limits of 35 miles per hour. The ominous clouds up ahead full of "tornadic" activity were amazing. Maybe I was high from the negative ions from the storm, but it was one of the happiest afternoons of my life.

VISITING MY PEOPLE 4

May 1, 2015

One of the things I love most about our great country is the sense of ownership and pride that our citizens have about where they live. For a politician or a comic, a guaranteed cheap applause line is to mention the city in which he or she is appearing. But woe be upon you, if you get it wrong! It is an affront from which you will not recover. Our emcee once called a comedy club full of NDSU students UND and we couldn't buy a laugh all night.

No matter how small the town, there is a green sign before the exit listing all the fabulous attractions the city fathers want you to know await you if you would please get out of your car, look around, and by all means, buy something. "See Our Old Round Barn!" one sign urges hopefully.

That rather reminded me of a "self-esteem building" exercise our son had to do in third grade. A piece of paper was passed around for each child and all the other children had to write anonymous morale-boosting things about that child. Several commented on what a good friend he was and how smart he was. But one child when pressed to come up with something positive, could only say, "Jacob has nice pants." How dramatically that affected the way our son esteemed himself I cannot say, but I'm sure it was decisive.

Some wit in Astoria, South Dakota, the town my mother and John Hinderaker's father grew up in, of some 237 hardy souls at its peak, has put up a green sign saying "Astoria, Next Four Exits."

If you don't stop at some of these things, the rest of your life could be one vast surging regret. You might miss the Sewer Cover Capital, or the World's Largest Ball of Twine, or a Corn Palace or Car Henge. Maybe it's not the Grand Canyon, The Alamo, or the Empire State Building, but, by golly, it's what the locals have to offer and they're proud. When I was a kid, I used to dream of being locked in the public library until I had read all the books. Now I dream of an endless road trip in which I see every single roadside attraction.

Other faded signs on the way into town trumpet a local sports team's long-ago accomplishments from the Girls' Softball team to the Boys' Basketball team. And coming soon to a town near you the Trans-Gender Rugby Tournament and Bake-Off!

This town sports a Spam museum; that one an Apothecary Museum; here a Runestone Museum; there a Quilt Museum and Shop with the hand-made sign: "Ladies, scream until your husband stops." The sweet, quaint assumption there being that the husband is driving and that every woman interested in quilts has one. A husband, not a quilt. Anyone can get a quilt. Here an Ostrich Ranch with but a single ostrich; there a herd of buffalo. Or goats. Or a longhorn whose name is probably Valium to sit upon for a photograph in Ft. Worth.

There's historic sites aplenty; homes of John Wayne, Jesse James, Laura Ingalls Wilder, more green signs mentioning astronauts and Olympians, golfers and NASCAR drivers. In Missouri you can't swing a cat without hitting a Harry S Truman statue, plaque, or memento.

If festivals are your cup of tea, you could opt for German Fest, Cajun Fest, a Barbecue Cook-off, Chuckwagon Cook-off, Krazy Daze.

The smallest town has a little park, valuable real estate set aside just for community pleasure and respite. Money is spent for sheer beautification. And has been, of course, since a lady living in the Lascaux cave in France looked at the wall and said, "You know what that wall needs, cher? Some pictures of our kids." And her husband said, "I can't draw people. How about some nice bison?" And then the neighbor lady asked her husband, "How come we don't have bison?" and the first interior decorator was born.

When a basket is functional, why waste any effort to also make it beautiful? But we humans do. Something within us compels us to make things pretty. And so it is in the small towns of my people. Seasonal decorations line the streets; flags fly from posts every few feet on the main drag. Often there are even Christmas decorations for perhaps a few more years before they are deemed Hate Speech along with American flags. Flower boxes surround somewhat shabby stores.

Even the old leftie song "Bread and Roses" about the 1911 Shirtwaist Factory Fire Disaster contained the line, "Hearts starve as well as bodies; give us bread, but give us roses." America is chock-a-block full of roses, actual and metaphorical. Stop and smell them.

VISITING MY PEOPLE 5

May 8, 2015

I was unable to leave any of my worldly goods strewn across the Heartland, like breadcrumbs pointing the way home. But not for lack of effort.

I have previously mentioned leaving my Nexus in Guthrie, Oklahoma — charging merrily away on the desk in my hotel room — with its Candy Crush and many beloved book titles on it — Donald E. Westlake in abundance, John D. McDonald, Vince Flynn, Lee Child – plus Power Line, Iowahawk, The Weekly Standard, Steynonline and Ace of Spades. I realized my error an hour down the road and considered returning but was loath to lose two hours in the effort. I called the hotel; they retrieved the Nexus from my room and held it in their safe for my return. Problem solved. It was undoubtedly a subconscious attempt to break the heroin-like grip that Candy Crush had on me. Sounds better than carelessness or stupidity.

Steeled in a new resolve to look after my belongings, I was baffled by the next mislaid object which happened to be my eyeglasses. Oh well, I reasoned, since I now had nothing to read anyway, to quote Madame Secretary, "What difference does it make at this point?" Besides, I had two backup pairs with me, only slightly more out-of-date than the lost pair. I tend to have annual medical exams of all kinds roughly every 8-10 years except for colonoscopies which I schedule without fail every 50. At least at eye exams they don't weigh you.

My distance vision is 20/10. If I hang the menu 21 feet away like a target, I can read it just fine. Alternatively, I could ask the server for his opinion and then I could be the one to say

"Excellent choice!" with enthusiasm. Not to brag, but, I'm batting 1.000 in making "excellent" choices in restaurants.

Apparently the glasses fell out of my always-attractive fanny pack (it's black and goes with anything...) when I inadvertently left a pocket unzipped. This occurred in the Ft. Worth Renaissance Hotel. They were not in the Lost and Found. But the next day, they just appeared on a table in a common area on the 8th floor! By that time I had picked up my travel companion for the last leg from Texas back to Arizona and she noticed the glasses and said, "Are these yours?" Woo-hoo! Two for two!

A Protestant minister acquaintance of mine had a devoutly religious mother whose zeal made him look like an atheist. Which judging by the number of SJW ministers I've known, he probably was. Anyhow, his mother believed fervently in all the saints and prayed to them regularly. She never traveled without St. Christopher, loyal even after his humiliating demotion. I learned that St. Anthony is the patron saint of lost objects and his mother would routinely look heavenward and yell, "Tony, Tony, look around! Something's lost and must be found!" Evidently, she was on a first-name, and even nickname basis with several of your top saints: Tony, Joey, Terri, Aggie, Francie, Petey, etc.

Well, Tony is a very ecumenical fellow, because he was on the look-out for a nice Jewish lady for 4500 miles.

Tony barely broke a sweat with the next incident. At the Smokestack Restaurant in Thurber, TX (pop. 5), my brain was bloated with THE best biscuits and gravy I had ever tasted. That, and possibly global warming, cooling, whatever, caused me to leave my cellphone on the table for only the second time in 10 years. But the waiter caught up with me before I had even finished paying at the cash register. Good gravy!! (Literally.) I was beginning to fear I could not travel any more without constant supervision. When I was a kid, I had all my mittens on strings. I need some kind of tether with everything attached and a taser to zap me gently when an item is off the string.

There was one final disturbing example wherein I THOUGHT I had left a favorite hoodie from my C2 Tactical Range in a restaurant just 200 miles from home – soooo close! – but it turned out I had put it in the trunk after all, so I choose not to count that one. In fact, I'm sorry I mentioned it, painting me as it does not just as distracted but slightly demented as well. Now don't you feel good about yourself? You're welcome.

If you guessed that when my BFF left Arizona after four more fun days of gabbing and shooting, she left HER cellphone in my car on the way to the airport, you would be correct. And she is eleven days younger than I am, though 8 minutes older than her twin. At the time of this writing we were on Day Three of a popular "overnight" carrier attempting to reunite her with it in a comedy of errors and incompetence, for once not mine. Saint Anthony, who was stressed out and fed up with us, was on a well-deserved vacation in Vegas. Luckily, nobody ever loses anything there. But watch out for the exercise equipment in Nevada. It'll put your eye out.

VISITING MY PEOPLE 6

May 15, 2015

Several weeks ago in this column, I set out on a journey to celebrate my parents' seventieth wedding anniversary back in my hometown in rural Minnesota. You have made the trip with me. As the sign says around construction zones: Thanks for your patience. The riots, scandals and terrorist attacks seemed to manage nicely without my take on them, but next week it's back to pithy political commentary. Can't have too much pith in troubled times.

What to make of such an amazing milestone? How do you log 70 years of marriage?

Steve Martin had a great old bit: How to make a million dollars and pay no taxes: "First, get a million dollars. Then, pay no taxes." (There was as yet no MSNBC to make that formula a reality.) Shhh…here's the secret: To attain such an impressive number of anniversaries, you have to get married pretty young and then try to live a very long time.

My father is a few weeks shy of 90; my mother, the cradle-robber, is 94. They have lived in Assisted Living for two years now. At the time of this writing, they were the only intact married couple there. So, in addition to your being quite old, your spouse has to be alive as well. Usually the men fail to hold up their end of that bargain. Soon after my 50th class reunion, the great guy who keeps us in touch emailed the sad news that four more classmates had passed, all of them men. In any nursing home, the ladies outnumber the men by about 8-1. C'mon, fellas, figure out how to live as long as we do. We love you and need you.

So, we're agreed that to reach 70 years of marriage, you must first live long and prosper. And then, of course – this is the tricky part — you have to stay together! This didn't used to be so hard because people just did it. Growing up, I never knew a single divorced person or young person with divorced parents until college. Back in the day, if there was a little window of happiness in a fairly miserable marriage, you stayed. Today it seems that if there is a little window of imperfection in a generally-happy marriage, you split up.

A friend of mine who has been through a boatload of therapy in his four marriages, introduced me to the concept of "co-dependence." I asked him, in all sincerity what the hell was wrong with that? It sounds like a good thing, but evidently, it's unhealthy in Therapy World. Who knew? Well, it worked for my parents.

They love each other very much. They have fun together. Mother is a very funny person who can always make Daddy laugh. Before her eyes degenerated, they did the crossword puzzle together every day. They enjoy Judge Judy, Wheel of Fortune, and FOX News. She loves clothes and always looks cute. A teeny person, her weight is exactly the same as her age! He is proud of his "arm candy." (My weight will only be the same as my age if I live to 125, which seems unlikely but is something to shoot for.)

My parents have always had a pretty rigid division of labor along traditional gender lines. He can't make instant oatmeal, though for decades he has insisted that he knows how to make Fudge. This Elusive Mystery Fudge has yet to appear but hope springs eternal. She was a spectacular cook; Her Greatest Hits include Rhubarb or Butterscotch Pie with flaky piecrust. Apple Turnovers from the apples Daddy lovingly raised in his fruit orchard. Fried Chicken to die for. Fresh Caramel Rolls floating off the plate for breakfast. My siblings and I are all pretty good cooks, mostly from having her food as a standard to live up to.

Daddy minds the investments and pays the bills; she cooked. She cleaned (and oh boy, did she clean); he fixed things. Everything worked perfectly in a spotless home. She raised us three kids, cleaned the store, and volunteered; he earned a nice living until he sold his drugstore and retired at an early age. She's never been a good "detail" person; he is meticulous with details. Co-dependence. Complementarity. A good thing. What did Rocky Balboa say about himself and Adrienne? "We fill gaps."

On the anniversary day, there was a festive reception at their Assisted Living facility. All the residents were invited whether or not they knew my parents' names, or even their own. Faye the Cook made a gorgeous cake and a handful of friends from around town came in. There were not nearly as many as attended Mother's big 70th birthday bash, already almost a quarter century ago. The downside of living that long is that you outlive most of your friends and many relatives. There were flowers, corsages, and ice cream to go with the cake. They got dozens of congratulatory cards, gifts and phone calls. Everybody with a cellphone snapped photos like paparazzi.

They were big-deal celebrities for nigh unto a week, including a human interest piece in the local paper. The dear little reporter – who has a great future in journalism – managed to get almost every detail in a brief article wrong, but still wrote a nice, if fanciful, little story.

Mr. Ammo Grrrll and I also married young. We have a nominal 22 years to go to celebrate our 70th. Heck, that's only about 8,000 shopping days left. May I suggest a nice Ed Brown 1911? Hope I can still rack the slide. Maybe you should just give it to me for our 48th in June. Yeah, that would be best I think. Why take chances?

MEA CULPA, MEA CULPA

May 22, 2015

Back in the early days of the Psychotic Ninny Wing of the feminist movement, now dominant, I read an article about a Men's Auxiliary of "supportive" men who stipulated to the premise that men were despicable. They opened each meeting by chanting "I am a lowly and abject turd." Surprisingly, this did not catch on as a mass phenomenon, but I now feel their pain.

It is possible that I, too, am some kind of noxious digestive waste product. For it is time for me to admit that for about 8 years, I read bedtime stories to my child! Yes, it's true and I offer self-incriminating visual evidence. In fact, I did not confine my reading just to bedtime, but sat him on my lap throughout the day and read to him from the age of 3 months. It continued long after the age of 3 when he could read himself.

And I did it without even once thinking about the callous indifference with which I was "disadvantaging" others! My parents had also disadvantaged my peers while they were living it up on $80 a month in college on the G. I. Bill. Par-tay!! Yes, they bought Little AG a brand new Golden Book twice a month (a quarter apiece), and read to me constantly, instilling a life-long passion for reading and learning. Oh, the humanity!

Isn't that amazing? Not only are people who read to their children merely "advantaging" their own. According to a moronic leftist college professor – but I repeat myself — these Haters are actively "disadvantaging" others. His ideal solution is to abolish the family, but he has a few kinks to work out there. He'll start with abolishing private school. (No matter. Unlike Obama and his kids, nobody in our family went there.) Oh, I hear you saying, "Sure Ms. Rich White Hetero Oppressor, you could afford books." Well, no.

We were poor as dirt, living in a two-bedroom flat in the Mission District in San Francisco where we rented out the second bedroom to single boarders. Except for continuing the tradition of a semi-monthly Golden Book (by then, over a dollar), we borrowed books from the public library. Which we walked to, since we did not own a car. On the rare occasions we required a car, my best friend drove. She had a car. She was a single mother on welfare.

The winter of 1974-5, the rainy season was particularly relentless. We couldn't get to Delores Park or the library for weeks. Somebody in our building put out a bundle of old magazines for the trash pickup and I took them and cut out pictures of dogs and kitties, cars and trucks, and pasted them on construction paper and made up stories to read to my little boy.

Every Tuesday was Free Day at the San Francisco Zoo. It cost a quarter for the trolley ride each way. Usually we brown-bagged it, but once a month I budgeted a dollar to squander on a hot dog to share with my toddler. One Terrible Tuesday (a day that will live in infamy) a seagull swooped down and stole that hot dog, our Precious. Oh, the crying, the shrieking! But eventually my 2-year-old got me calmed down.

The neighborhood center had Baby Gym once a week wherein the tots were encouraged to jump off little ramps onto mattresses and hang on what were surely germ-factory rings. Cost? Bupkiss, nada. Can't read? Group Story Time at the library was also free.

So, in addition to reading to him myself, I thought it important to provide modest cultural and physical enrichment, none of which cost a dime. No amount of "income inequality" figured into it at all. I had a husband – the excellent Mr. Ammo Grrrll – and he had a job. But after taxes, we barely netted more than my friend got on assistance and food stamps. We paid rent; she lived with her mother. By the way, as my co-conspirator, Mr. AG read to our son too. I want to make that abundantly clear so we can be cellies at re-education camp.

Class envy peddlers like Mr. Krugman, Princess Cheekbones Warren, President No Private School for Thee, Just Me, and all of that fake-populist millionaire crowd are just dead wrong. It is ALL about personal responsibility, values, and culture. If successful middle class people in general, and Asians and Jews in particular, have historically valued scholastic endeavors more than some cultures, embrace that. Emulate it. If we spent every discretionary penny on educational opportunities for our child instead of cigarettes, tattoos, Air Jordans, or even pretty basic consumer goods, I'm not sorry.

Generations of self-sacrificing African-American parents worshiped education as the way up from poverty and millions succeeded through education, courage, and hard work. If "turning over in one's grave" were a reality, the deceased ancestors of the droopy-drawered, "education is a white thang" idiots would surely be a new source of energy.

Oh, and the aforementioned welfare mother? We moved back to Minnesota; she took a medical-coding course while on assistance. She got a good job, and saved up for a down payment on a tiny condo far from our degenerating neighborhood. It had gotten so bad that she had grocery bags stolen from her car while she was carrying the first two bags into the apartment. Our park became an open-air drug bazaar.

She worked the rest of her life till retirement. Today her son is a wealthy video-game artist living in a multi-million-dollar mansion in San Francisco. It has a 360 degree view of the Bay Area including the sketchy neighborhood where two determined young mothers read to their beautiful little boys.

PSYCHOTIC NINNIES, CIRCA 1975

May 29, 2015

Last Friday I referred to the Psychotic Ninny Wing of the feminist movement. In the beginning they were a relatively small part of the legitimate push for equality and expanded opportunities for women. But they always existed. In a meeting I attended in 1970, a certifiably insane woman waxed rhapsodic about how "when we hang all the men they will emit sperm and we can collect that and reproduce without men." The logistics of that scenario alone were daunting and the image tough to erase. I thought, "Holy crap! I will sit here quietly and hope her spaceship picks her up soon!"

I'm about to describe another incident which was an early precursor to the hoaxes, disgusting "rape culture" slander and tedious anti-male bigotry on campus today. Since virtually every legal equality has already been won, and the saner feminists have retired from the field, victorious, the lunatic fringe has more influence in a smaller pond.

It is ever thus in every "social justice" movement. The more obvious it becomes that virtually all impediments to success have been removed, the more furious the professional "victims" become that nothing much has changed in their lives. And the more resentful of others whose life decisions and discipline have catapulted them to success.

Individual success is anathema to a victim class. It does not inspire; it refutes the linchpin of their victimhood: that the deck is permanently stacked against them all. Those who profit from their professional victim status cling to it like a Titanic survivor to a piece of driftwood. Michelle Obama springs to mind: an obscenely-rich professional vacationer and Food Scold who claims to be dissed at Target and unwelcome at museums in the racist country that elected her unqualified, incompetent husband. Twice.

On the particular day I would like to discuss, my friend and I wheeled our toddlers toward Castro Street and decided to stop in to a women's coffeehouse for a cup of herbal tea. Though The Full Moon called itself a coffeehouse for women, it was only for the right kind.

We quickly became aware that all the other women were what Robin Williams called "women in comfortable shoes" and what I called "The Hairy Armpit Crew." Now, I am completely neutral on whatever people's personal preferences are for body hair. I'm told that some men even find it appealing. Whatever. But in the early '70s, not shaving your legs or armpits became a STATEMENT, a furry I.D. Badge for being at minimum a radical feminist.

My friend and I were clearly breeders, our Strollers of Shame advertising our cavorting with the enemy. The hostility could be cut with a knife. We got our tea and sat down. Within minutes, a large unhappy woman with the mandatory bushy armpits and a crewcut approached us and asked about our babies. "Are those *boys*?" she fairly spat. Both toddlers had longish curls and were – in my utterly unbiased opinion – extraordinarily good-looking.

We admitted that they were boys. She then ordered us to leave because – and who could forget such a statement even 40 years later? – "some of the women are feeling rape vibes."

I'm pretty sure there must have been a time in my life when I was more enraged, but I can't think of when it might have been.

My friend, of a less combative nature, immediately got up and fled, expecting I was behind her. I stayed put. Cursed with a slavish devotion to Logic, I said, "If you had to ASK if these were boys, those vibes must have been pretty weak. I paid for this tea. If you want me gone, you'd best call the cops. I am going to finish my tea with my beautiful boy and if you touch one hair on his head, you will find yourself in court. After you come out of your coma."

It was a ludicrous threat; the woman was twice my size and I had a baby with me, never an asset in a donnybrook. But, being a very small person, I was forced to learn at an early age that bullies are always caught off guard when you fight back. She looked into my eyes, and wisely chose to stomp back to her coven. Like Mean Girls everywhere, they resumed looking daggers at me.

It's not easy to drink Red Zinger when you're shaking like a leaf. But I dragged it out as long as I could. And left, with as much dignity as could be mustered by a person on the verge of stroking out. When I was a few feet from the door, I yelled, "If you hate men so much, how come you are trying so hard to look like one?" Mind you, I was a card-carrying left-wing Democrat at the time. But you don't associate my 18-month-old baby boy with the worst crime after murder and expect me to just take it and slink away.

I do not know if that den of discrimination is still there; I suspect not. Most establishments don't last for 40 years. But anti-male bigotry lives on and thrives. Now it is backed up by the giant truncheon of the state. On campus, at the highest reaches of multi-culti government, The Psychotic Ninnies and their pet eunuchs rule. It is long past time to fight back.

Trigger warning: Run! Or grab your Teddy Bear or Play-Doh.

Here are the scary boy babies who invaded the Safe Space for Psychotic Ninnies.

CAMPAIGN SLOGANS

June 6, 2015

FYEO: Reply All. Top Secret DNC Memo From Debbi Wasserman-Test Schultz

Leaked by the Norks

It appears that Hillary is in freefall and we may need some kind of backup plan in case the campaign season entails her actually having to appear in public sometime in the next 17 months. And Gawd forbid, having to answer questions. So, am in process of designing multimedia campaign for alternatives. Need slogans for all candidates, plus an overall theme. Remember, we're spitballin' here – no bad ideas. We will undoubtedly never equal Hope and Change for vague words people like that have one syllable. (What are you "Hoping" for? What's gonna "Change"? Nobody asked!! Amazing! Let's repeat that, people!)

Though some of these words have multiple syllables, they all tested well in focus groups. People liked Puppies and Porn; but Cupcakes and Free Shit did best of all. Trying to get artist who designed halo for Dear Leader to do a nifty cupcake.

Here are a few ideas for our first group of possible candidates. More will follow:

ELIZABETH

With Dear Leader calling her just by her first name, we are thinking that must be cool. Like, you know, Yanni, Cher, Sting. Fabian. Campaign slogans:

Elizabeth: Come for the Uterus; Stay For The High Cheek Bones!
Elizabeth: Just As Radical as Bernie and Not a White Man!
Elizabeth: Remember How Well It Went With the Last One-Term Senator?
Elizabeth: She'll carry Massachusetts and Minnesota!

Campaign Song: "Cherokee Maiden" by Willie Nelson. Many have suggested that a country singer could peel off votes from the Crazy Gun Nut Redneck Taliban Wing of the Republican party. (Not that I'm suggesting in any "high horse" kinda way that the Taliban are as bad as the Tea Party; they are just unemployed, not evil.)

JOHN and AL

Then there are our two loser retreads, perhaps re-branded successfully? Cost savings on leftover yard signs. Duct tape over non-persons, Joe L. and John E.

Campaign Slogans:

Kerry: He's The Bomb!
Kerry: A Swift Boat to Prosperity.
Kerry: Anyone with a Yacht, an $8,000 bike and Wacky Condiment Queen Billionaire Wife understands your problems!
Kerry: He's Got One of Them Thar Huntin' Licenses.

Campaign Theme Songs should remind voters of John's invaluable service as a player in the negotiations to give Iran a nuclear weapon. In honor of that landmark accomplishment, we are working on a deal with – are you sitting down? – the Eagles for a medley of hits including "Wasted Time," "Lyin' Eyes," and

"Desperado"!! I'm sure you're as excited as I am. Someone has also suggested Merle Haggard's "My Own Kind of Hat," but we think the Eagles' medley has broader appeal.

Word up: Nobody should return John Edwards's relentless phone calls. Caller Reject, people.

As a last resort, we could try Al again. He also has billions of dollars. Can afford to travel with a snowplow and sand truck to deal with unfortunate blizzards wherever he appears. This is particularly embarrassing in July. Earth tone wardrobe may need to be let out.

GORE: Because Everyone Loves a Rich Old Bloated Hysteric
GORE: Data, Schmata! It's Getting Warmer!
GORE: Forget, Hell! I'm Still Mad About 2000. I Won, Dammit.

Now, here we also have two suggestions for a Campaign Theme Song. "Growing Older But Not Up" by Jimmy Buffett and "I'd Like to Have That One Back" by George Strait. We would love to get Paul McCartney on board with "Here Comes the Sun," but that could mistakenly associate the sun with warmer temps. As if.

In the event that Hillary does not go gentle into that good night, here are a few more possible slogans to push her Reset Button, as it were:

Hillary: Go To The Back of the Line!
Hillary: It's my TURN, dammit!
Hillary: All Those "Donors" Are Gonna Be Pissed If They Don't Get What They Paid For!
And finally, for the sympathy vote that won her the Senate in

**New York:
Hillary: Her Husband Cheats!**

Campaign theme song which we feel celebrates the whole Clinton power couple: Dire Straits' "Money For Nothing and Chicks For Free."

Debbi

SHLEPPING TOWARDS UTOPIA

June 12, 2015

Well, Mattress Girl has evidently graduated from Columbia. In Electrical Engineering, I think. Ha, ha, I kid. Of course it was "Visual Arts." (Though in fairness, she considered Physics.) Heck, I was a Sociology major, so talk about "High Horse" Syndrome! And she finished in four years whereas it took me three terms: Johnson's, Nixon's, and Carter's. So kudos to Mattress Girl. I'm guessing she intends to schlep this mattress from here all the way to Assisted Living. It's a great gig.

I know Mattress Girl's name is Emma, but she has been given quite enough publicity and accolades for her specious tale, and I choose to refer to her as MG.

MG was allowed to drag her 50-lb mattress across the stage with the help of three confederates. What a festive and dignified occasion! I believe that Dr. Thomas Sowell once described college administrators as a crossbreed of a jellyfish and a parrot. That MG was allowed to do this speaks volumes about how we got to this state of affairs. When I went to college, we were introduced to the concept of "in loco parentis," Latin for "in place of parents." That meant they not only looked out for us, but occasionally had to slap us upside the head. But nowadays college administrators would be better described by more of a loose Spanish translation of those words – "batcrap crazy loco parents."

Let's review the facts as determined by both the police and a school review process highly tilted in favor of the accuser. MG apparently participated in a variety of consensual sex acts with a German scholarship student and then the insensitive assailant didn't even call afterwards despite her many texts. These facts aside, she still gets to spend a year lugging the mattress around campus and also to make a distracting spectacle of herself at graduation and ruin the occasion for everyone else.

So I am proposing that in the future, EVERYBODY gets to schlep some totem across the stage at graduation. It would provide badly-needed exercise for our obese youth.

Everyone should think hard about some traumatic event and then find something to lug. No traumatic events in your 22 or so years, graduates? Well, for heaven's sake, make something up! You, too, could win an all-expenses-paid trip to the State of the Union Address. Personally, I would sooner clean the men's room in a Greyhound Bus Station. But the point is if you make up something good enough – spending thousands of dollars on birth control, being assaulted by an entire fraternity or sports team – you will get a lot of attention.

Even when your preposterous tale is debunked, you will still be referred to as The Sacred Victim and the debunkers virally vilified. So there's really no downside.

So let's think of objects to represent your angst. Let me get the ball rolling with some suggestions drawn from my own life of relentless oppression. When I was eight years old, I wanted a bicycle in the worst way. My best friend got a beautiful new blue Schwinn for Christmas. My parents were too thrifty to spring for a new bike. Mother found a used one at a garage sale and Daddy painted it a flat non-metallic red. I was very disappointed, but would have cut out my tongue before I hurt my parents' feelings.

But that is the kind of item that could be carried or even ridden across the stage at a graduation ceremony. No joyful wheelies though! Remember, you are enraged and depressed at all times.

Never let anything go, that's the secret to the good life.

In the eighth grade I also sewed a hideous skirt in Home Economics. I received the only "C" in my entire academic career until Physical Geography in college. If only I had thought to shlep a Singer Sewing Machine of Misery across the stage. Maybe in a little wagon behind the Bike of Invidious Comparison.

Are you a guy who never got off the bench of the JV squad? (we're talking football here, not ISIS). You could carry a Tackling Dummy of Deprivation. Fat people could carry A Doctor's Scale of Humiliation.

Graduation ceremonies already take longer than an Oscar telecast emceed by Obama with a broken Teleprompter, a totally "uh-some" speaker. So having everyone also schlep iconic items with them could turn the ceremonies into eventual sleepovers. Then you'll be sorry that you chose a scale instead of a mattress! This year, mattresses; next year, full-size floats.

I apologize for the jarring change of tone. But I want to make one final, extremely unfunny point. The mattress fails utterly even as Artistic Metaphor. I have known three women who were raped for real. One was attacked in a parking lot; one was taken hostage and attacked in the woods; one was left for dead by three illegals in a home invasion.

Nobody got a mattress.

A woman with a perpetual mattress on her back is an almost perfect metaphor not for "rape culture," but for the empty misery of the hookup culture. Billy Crystal famously said, "A woman needs a reason to have sex; a man just needs a place." So in MG's world, women are even toting the "place" with them wherever they go. Just in case? Young women voluntarily climb into bed with young men they barely know, who do not love them, and then find that it wasn't the empowering fun-fest that was advertised. Why are so many drugs and a sea of alcohol necessary to get through an experience sometimes quaintly referred to as "making love"? This hookup culture is an unmitigated disaster on every level. For women, to be sure, but for their sandbagged partners and for our culture as well.

GOD BLESS THE DADDIES

June 19, 2015

Sunday, of course, is Father's Day. Despite decades of being portrayed in sitcoms and commercials as brainless twits who would be lost without the superior intelligence of their eye-rolling wives and children, the true importance of fathers can scarcely be overstated. If you doubt me, visit any prison jammed to bursting with lost fatherless men.

In our neighborhood in the 50s and 60s, the fathers were the stuff of small-town life: shopkeepers, house painters, teachers, ministers, highway patrolmen, traveling salesmen, car salesmen, insurance adjusters, mechanics and carpet-layers. Several of my parents' best friends were farmers, although, needless to say, they lived on farms.

They were Old School Daddies who did not change diapers except under the greatest duress – the wife in hospital with the plague, or another baby – nor did they share housework. They worked; for most professions, that was more or less dawn to dusk, including weekends. My Dad had 3 Sundays off a month. It was one of life's great mysteries what the T.V. Daddies did who had the ability to hang around the house all day playing tricks on "the gals" with the other indolent husbands.

If my neighborhood housed great intellectuals, they were well hidden. Which doesn't at all mean they weren't smart guys. They knew all kinds of useful stuff. But, very few of us get a father who is or was a towering intellectual giant – an Irving Kristol, say, a Victor Davis Hanson, a WFB. Nor were most of our daddies universally-respected pillars of the community like my friend Angela's father, John O. Smith, who had over 1,000 people at his funeral, or Irving Hinderaker (what is it about the name Irving?) such that they are inducted into a community Hall of Fame.

This is a paean just to the average, responsible guy who tries his best. To the Daddy who is there for the 1-0 soccer matches in the rain, and also at the dance recitals which should by law come with an infinity symbol on the program. To the Daddy who goes to work every workday and comes home every night to eat dinner. Or breakfast, if he works graveyard. To the Daddy who teaches manliness to his sons and what to look for in a man to his daughters.

Author Jillian Churchill has famously said, "There is no way to be a perfect mother; and a million ways to be a good one." Thank God for all our good fathers, even the ones who are as disappointingly human at times as we ourselves are. Even Tony Soprano was allowed to have "issues." Nobody gets out of this vale of tears unscathed. My father's whole family was shattered by the loss of the oldest son in battle in the Pacific. Unless you're talking about shutting an actual door, "closure" is a silly made-up word. There is no such thing, only coping.

My bedroom was in the partially-finished basement of our home. One night in about the 4th grade I had a terrible nightmare and woke up convinced that a very bad monster was in my room. I screamed bloody murder and Daddy ran downstairs in about 10 seconds. He looked everywhere for the bad guy with a flashlight, hugged me, and I was able to go back to sleep because Daddy was on the job. He wasn't that imposing physically, and though we had deer rifles and shotguns, we never had a handgun in the house. But he was Daddy and there was no doubt that he was in charge. Only the most foolhardy of monsters would dare to take him on! We were safe. And safe is essential in a perilous world.

I have never read anything more beautiful or moving than Jonah Goldberg's eulogy for his late father, Sid Goldberg, called "The Hop Bird." Google it if you haven't read it. Bring tissues. But few of us get the brilliant, wise, humorous father who always says exactly the perfect thing. The daddies in my neighborhood said things more along the lines of "Don't make me stop this car." Or, "Stop crying, or I'll give you something to cry about," and that wasn't all bad either. I have been maintaining for years, with all the hullaballoo about "bullying" – as though that's a brand-new, hitherto undiscovered thing! – that we don't need more "zero tolerance" rules; we need tougher, more resilient kids.

Daddy taught me to bait a hook, to golf, to hit a baseball, throw a spiral, to mow the grass. To work 12 hours a day in a drugstore, wait on customers pleasantly, asking "May I help you?" and count back their change the old-fashioned way. To save money and eschew debt. To be on time, which he defined as 10 minutes early.

And despite the ludicrous feminist contention that little girls of the era were forcibly prevented from playing with blocks and herded behind razor wire into the doll corner in school, neither he nor any teacher ever made me feel that there was anything I couldn't do or accomplish because I was a girl. There were four of us in the Class of '64 who shared valedictory honors: three girls and just one boy, who was also my debate partner. No Affirmative Action; no disparate impact; no IX or any other Titles required. Just high expectations and effort.

Perhaps most important, Daddy taught me to fight back. To defend myself and others from bullies. He made me assertive enough to defend my beliefs, which always seemed to be at odds with popular thought. I thank Daddy for that contrarian spirit, and hundreds of other things. He is almost 90 now, and last time I visited and took him and Mom out for Chinese, they had a minor argument on the way about whether they were sharing Cashew Chicken or Orange Beef. And I was able, at last, to say to him, "Don't make me stop this car." And then add, "Heck, let's just get both."

Happy Father's Day, good daddies, one and all.

YES MEANS YES

June 26, 2015

Writer Ashe Schow of the Washington Examiner has an excellent column about the proposed new "Yes Means Yes" law from two Law Professors who definitely need a hobby. Google it for facts and details. The gist of it is to make virtually every sexual encounter rape, unless "affirmative consent" can be proved for each and every stage of the event. And if you married guys think you are going to get a pass, you are sadly mistaken.

How "yes" can be proved without either videotaping or getting signed documents from the parties is beyond me, but what I want to discuss is not the specifics of the law, but the changes such a bill would entail in areas that perhaps have not been thought through.

Every year, billions and billions of "bodice-ripping" Romance Novels are written, published and consumed like salted peanuts. At least it seems like billions when I am stuck in an airport looking for a book to read on the plane and this is all that is on offer. I have read exactly one in my entire life. I gather it wasn't supposed to be a comedy, but I found it hilarious both for its Victorian reluctance to mention clinical names for either body parts or sex acts, and the overwrought prose.

Here is my take on the new improved genre after Yes Means Yes becomes law.

Samantha gazed at Haven as he lifted the log off her sprained ankle. His rippling muscles tore the buttons right off his shirt, drawn rather too tightly across his surprisingly-hairless chest, if the cover photo is to be believed. One of the buttons got caught in Haven's long golden hair, which is almost a mullet, only cooler, obviously, and not at all gay.

Samantha felt an ache. In her ankle, of course, which we mentioned earlier was sprained. But also in her nether regions. She had never wanted anything as much in her life as she wanted Haven's throbbing man-thing. Well, except for wanting that cannoli the time she was on Atkins and was really sick of meat and eggs and cheese. Oh God, why can't we have World Peace, and why can't carbs make you thinner, she wondered aloud?

Haven pressed her bee-stung ruby lips against his chest, in part to get her to stop talking. This was a definite intrusion into her Safe Space, and illegal according to the Law Of No Touching, but Samantha was willing to stipulate that it was fine. She could always change her mind later if Haven gave her a crappy birthday gift or something.

Neither nether region had stopped throbbing so Haven pulled Samantha even closer, as close as he could get what with the throbbing and all, and whispered romantically, "May I touch your left bosom? I'm right-handed and that would be easier."

"Yes, yes! For God's Sake, get on with it!" she said breathlessly. But no. Haven was no fool. His cousin, Heathcliff, got kicked out of college for failing to mention his fiancée's left thigh on the Permission List and he was taking no chances. He then went through the entire mandatory inventory of other body parts as Samantha tried to remember if she had left her iron on, and dreamed of the cannoli.

When, at last, Haven had received permission to touch the other bosom, each arm, her nose, each ear, her lady bits, shins, *ankles and toes, and had given his Notary Public the GPS coordinates to find them in the woods, Samantha found that she had mostly lost interest.*

"Let's just cuddle," she said and pouted prettily when she realized that Haven did not appear to be overly disappointed.

Clearly, this will also impact porn.

Act One, Scene 1: A livingroom with minimal furniture and shag carpeting. Four hard-looking, bored women who look like they have never read a book in their lives are gathered for "Book Club," wearing highly unlikely outfits for a book club gathering. They are drinking white wine, which, as any fool knows, must be chilled and – oh, no! – the refrigerator is on the fritz. What a clever plot twist! Luckily, the hostess has the refrigerator repairman on speed dial.

The refrigerator repairman arrives at once and not in the typical nine-five time frame, almost as though he was waiting right outside. He has also brought three buddies of various races with him. It must be a union shop with flagrant feather-bedding and diversity requirements for government contracts.

The repairmen pay scant attention to the fridge and get right down to business removing their clothing, as your less reliable repairmen sometimes will tend to do. From the looks of the toolbox, apparently there was a misunderstanding about what "Bonded" meant. Then they take out their long, long, uh, lists and ask, in unison, "May I touch your…"

Much, much later the women all cry at one of Oprah's recommended books – a mendacious howler about Several Cups of Tea – and drink a great deal of warmish white wine.

JULY, AUGUST, and SEPTEMBER

When the average "crisis cycle" in news today is about 3 days – well, except for the weeks-long discussion of the current President's private parts and years-long Russian collusion delusion – it is sometimes hard to remember what was going on at any given time.

Hopefully, these columns will jog your memory. Which is the only body part of mine that jogs. Besides, a number of light humorous entries that I hope you will enjoy, there will be reference to the drive to put some historical figure who is not a white man on money, a parody of President Obama's wretched "negotiations" with Iran, more on the kangaroo courts on campus, and two decidedly un-funny, but important pieces on Planned Parenthood's subsidiary industry of selling baby parts, and the unfortunate and totally-preventable tragedy of Michael Brown's death.

The September 18 column recounts my dear mother's terrible fall at her Assisted Living place. She was 94 at the time, sharp as a tack, and didn't even use a walker. For so many seniors, a fall robs them of what was left of their mobility and begins a steep and rapid decline, especially if the senior has sustained head injuries as well. For Mother, this fall was indeed the beginning of the end of her long and beautiful life. Fortunately, we did not know that for sure at the time.

Re-reading that column makes me very sad because now I know how it comes out. Of course, "it is what it is" as the true, but irritating, slogan goes; and the grieving for her is well into its third year at this writing. There is, in my opinion, no such thing as "closure", only coping. So, on we go, doing the best we can to wrest maximum joy from each and every day. That is how

Mother lived her life and how she would want her family and friends to carry on.

She loved country music. Her two very favorite songs in the world were Nat King Cole's "Mona Lisa" and "Waltz Across Texas" by Ernest Tubb with Willie Nelson and friends lending a hand. So, let's close out this season of columns with a rip-roaring defense of country music. As only country music can express adequately, Life goes on, in all its comedy and tragedy; farce and satire, love and hate; fidelity and betrayal; good dogs, good women, and bad whiskey. What a ride!

THE THRIFTY TEXAN

July 3, 2015

The Paranoid Texan is my regular morning walking partner whenever the temperature in our Dusty Little Village is lower than body temperature. We have our limits, even here in Arizona. Mr. Ammo Grrrll is a runner, not a walker, plus he runs with headphones in which he is hearing and repeating Hebrew dialogue as he runs. Which is not companionable, but does complete the picture along with his running outfit, of making him resemble a recently escaped mental patient. The outfit includes a bush hat which, when anchored by the headphones, turns into a *Little House on the Prairie* style bonnet.

I have heard many people say, "I don't care what other people think of me." Most of them are lying. Mr. AG truly does not care if he is hip or cool. He cares if people think he is honest, ethical and kind. Beyond that, he doesn't mind channeling Laura Ingalls Wilder if she had up and left her little house on the prairie and moved to a little kibutz in Israel.

So, one day, I go to collect the PT for our walk and he informs me that he's sorry that he can't go because he spent the entire previous day either on Hold, or talking with a variety of bureaucrats at a motley assemblage of insurance companies and HR departments in order to save $1,000. A goodly amount of money and well worth a day's effort, no matter how tedious.

He had only one tiny part of that task left, he said. Today, he was fixin' to spend just four hours to save $9.00 on some refresher driving class for seniors. I offered to GIVE him a ten-spot (which only has an old dead white guy on it, anyway) and said he could even keep the change. I'll probably win it back at the next poker game. He insisted it wasn't about the money, but there was some cockamamie principle involved. A "principle" that involves working for a little over $2.00 an hour?

"What about the principle of committing to exercise so we don't turn into the dreaded roly-poly Walmartians?"

"One day won't make any difference in that." The Paranoid Texan has the strongest resistance to being ripped off of anyone I have ever known, except for Mr. Ammo Grrrll.

Mr. AG's bargaining skills have made grown car salesmen cry. I also witnessed a memorable conversation in the Sears Home and Garden Department when we bought our first modest home. When we moved into the house one cold April day in Minnesota, we bought the most basic electric lawn mower Sears had on offer.

The salesman had started with a riding John Deere that cost more than either of our crap cars and reluctantly worked his way down. The only grass-cutter more basic than what we selected would have been a Garden Weasel or, possibly, a goat.

He then tried to sell the young Mr. AG a year-long "extended warranty" for about half of what we had just paid for the lawn mower. "A year?" asked Mr. AG, with hardly a trace of sarcasm. "That should come in handy in Minnesota from October through next April."

When The Paranoid Texan lopes down to the mailboxes, he often stops by our house to get our mailbox key too. So we have had occasion to open our electric and water bills at the same time. This month our electric bill was exactly double his! I was pretty sure it was blatant anti-Semitism, and not the fact his identical house is dark except for the room he is currently in, while I keep mine well-lit enough to guide small aircraft to a safe night landing within.

Being a Texan, he also has his air conditioning set to 86, whereas if I accidentally left the milk out for a couple days, it would be perfectly safe. Once when we lived in an apartment on the East Side of St. Paul, Mr. Ammo Grrrll took me somewhat forcefully by the arm into the basement to see all the electric meters ticking slowly away, save for one. In Apartment 107, it appeared that the meter was actually spinning. Uh-oh. That can't be good. Must be defective.

The PT is far from poor. But he believes buying food is a waste. Especially if it has to be cooked, which squanders electricity. He is not a fussy eater. One of his favorite meals is tacos from Jack In The Box – that famous purveyor of fine Mexican food – six for $3.23. He asks: Is it fast? Is it easy? Can it be microwaved?

Sometimes he also asks if it's cheap, but fast and easy are more important. He eats on paper plates. In the dark, he says. (He rarely accepts our nearly daily dinner invitation, because usually – catch this, ladies – he says he is "not hungry." Like hunger has anything at all to do with eating!)

But back to our topic: What is it about guys and fear of somebody taking advantage of them? Maybe we women are just used to it.

A multimillionaire friend of mine pitched a fit when we had lunch in a popular Mall of America restaurant that charged a $1.00 apiece "mixology" charge to mix two cocktails. He never returned. ("Well done, management! Lose a customer over $2.00!")

And that was about the same time he donated $10 Million Dollars to the University of Minnesota for scholarships. So, clearly, he was not cheap. He just refused to be ripped off. "Millions for defense; not one penny for tribute," and all that.

Friends: Under what circumstances would you spend four hours to save $9.00? Discuss. Show your work.

TEN-DENTIOUS

July 10, 2015

Oh, God. Make it stop; make it stop. We are $18 bazillion quadrillion in debt (seriously, I looked it up...), half added since Dear Leader has been in charge. Obamacare accomplished absolutely none of the promised benefits ("Cover 40 Million people! Bend the Cost Curve! Keep your Insurance If You Like It! No Illegals, Except for the Illegals Who Don't Have Insurance!") in exchange for destroying the best health care delivery system in the world.

Millions upon millions of Federal employees are vulnerable to identity theft, blackmail, threats, at least four times as many people as the Administration admitted to at first.

Dear Leader is trying his best to lose against our beheading, gay-murdering, woman-mutilating enemies in the Middle East, but as slowly as possible so as to leave the biggest, most intractable mess for the next person in charge. The timing is tricky. If he's not careful, Iran will have the bomb before Dear Leader is out of office. I'm sure it's part of the backdoor deal to wait until January 21, 2017 to fire one at Israel. Was ensuring that Iran gets the bomb the ultimate pricetag for this Man-Choom-ian Candidate to pay back his consigliere, Valerie Jarrett, who was born there? She made the Obamas rich beyond any possible dreams of obscene avarice even before the post-Presidential loot rolls in like a tsunami.

Speaking of Dreamers, they continue to stream across the open border along with all their relatives, and assorted Nightmares in the form of drug dealers, drug users, murderers, rapists and terrorists, and one quarter of all of Mexico. All waiting for Food Stamps, welfare, schools for their children, and Driver's Licenses that will allow them to register to vote.

A record number of Americans are not in the workforce. Millions are newly "disabled" in order to get large checks that were never intended to go to the "depressed." A friend of mine is a Social Security appeals judge. She said one man who had been turned down at a lower level said he needed Disability because everyone else in his family was on it and he felt he wasn't doing his part.

We wouldn't even know where to start to turn this around, even if either party had the political will, which neither does. And what is an absolutely critical task before us? Besides hounding sports teams with Indian names, I mean? Replacing Alexander Hamilton on the 10-spot with A Woman. Any Woman. It reminds me of when my house is a disaster, the column is unwritten, and I decide it's urgent to alphabetize my spices.

If it's the 10, why not Bo Derek? She's beautiful, accomplished, and a Republican. But, I guess she has to be dead, too. The Paranoid Texan suggested Marilyn Monroe, the pic with the skirt blowing up, and allowed as how he would probably carry more tens in that case.

We can see this grotesque process unfolding. Why stop with just a plain old ordinary dead woman? What about blacks, gays, Hispanics, transgendered, disabled, Asians and Jews (ha! As if...)? Can you imagine the hue and cry if it's a white woman? Of course it won't be. So, let's get the whole pc crapfest over with and make sure she's a gay black woman. Comedian Wanda

Sykes maybe. She seems nice. Of course, she's also alive, so that's a problem.

One thing is sure. No woman, no matter how accomplished, no matter her contribution, will be as important to the country as Alexander Hamilton. As Paul Mirengoff pointed out, damn few men could equal his contribution. But no matter. Not one person in 1000 could even name his contributions without Wikipedia. Just another old dead white guy. A President, maybe? Yeah, the one after Ben Franklin.

But who will be chosen to build on the raging success of the Susan B. Anthony dollar? Sacajawea was returned to her tribe by Lewis and Clark, white male explorers, after being kidnapped by another tribe of Indians. Kidnapped? By other Indians? Say what?! Oopsy.

Either Rosa Parks or Harriet Tubman is my best guess for who it will be. Both women of great valor to be sure, and what I liked best about Tubman was that she always carried a gun. Uh-oh. Bad, bad, bad. How will they get around this? Well, hell, just LIE about it.

She's the wrong color, but my vote for the perfect woman to capture the spirit of our beloved country after 40 years of Pravda-worthy propaganda and culminating in 8 years of this wretched regime: Calamity Jane. A hopeless binge drinker who wasn't even a good marksman like Annie Oakley, a woman who invented or embellished most of her accomplishments. As I said, perfect. And still nicer than any woman or man in this Administration.

NEGOTIATING 101

July 17, 2015

I have been married to Mr. Ammo Grrrll for 48 happy years. God forbid anything should happen to this marriage, but if it should, I want Barack Hussein Obama and John FibSwiftboat Kerry to be the attorneys for my husband.

Me: I want the house in Arizona and both cars. Plus alimony of $10 million a month. In gold. I need to buy a lot more guns. A lot. He can have the Papa Murphy coupons, all science fiction, and any souvenir t-shirts or caps mentioning the Chicago Cubs. I need substantial child support as well.

HBO/JK: Fine. We are just hunky-dory with that. We weren't aware you had a little dependent child.

Me: He's 42. Still on my insurance under Obamacare's newest extension. I also want the house in Minnesota and all the CDs. Also the CD player.

HBO/JK: Sounds fair to us. Apparently, the CD player is the one technological device you can actually operate. We do fail to grasp why anyone would live in Minnesota. Have you seen Fargo, for Pete's sake?

Me: Be that as it may. I need my 401K, of course, but I want his too. It's quite a bit bigger than mine.

HBO/JK: We see no problem with that.

HBO/JK: We would like to inspect your checkbook and portfolio to make sure you aren't hiding any assets that would normally be part of community property. You know, if we could. Please.

Me: Inspections? Are you crazy? Inspections were never on the table. No. Death to you, Great Satan, and Satan Mini-Me.

HBO/JK: Well, OK, then, we give up. Don't say we didn't try.

Me: As well you should give up, you sons of pigs and dogs.

HBO/JK: We see that you are holding his four boxes of baseball cards hostage. Could we possibly mention that he would like those back before we conclude here?

Me: No.

HBO/JK: You seem bitter and angry even though you've won. Will you promise not to kill him any earlier than 10-15 years from now?

Me: Absolutely.

HBO/JK: You do know, right, that crossing your fingers is childish and does not invalidate this negotiation that 99% of the whole wide world supports?

Me: Neener, neener.

HBO/JK: Well, guess we're done here. Another successful settlement. Where's our Peace Prize?

MS. MANNERS FOR PLANNED NON-PARENTHOOD FLAKS

July 24, 2015

Sometimes when a Cosmo Girl of Today has lunch with pals, sipping an amusing little glass of merlot, the question of what to talk about arises. The old admonition against sex, religion, and politics, is, of course, laughingly out of date. Still, there are some topics to be avoided, particularly if food is involved.

Body parts are fine if you are referencing Courageous Caitlyn's cleavage. Or Kim Kardashian's kapacious kaboose. (What IS it with that family and why does anyone else CARE???) Or chatty vaginas having adorable monologues. Those body parts are of general interest to everyone, especially those famous pictures of Kim's kaboose covered with half the sand from the Sahara. Tasteful and topical! Or is that tacky but tropical?

But talking about selling baby livers, hearts and limbs, Ms. Manners feels, should only be done in a non-food setting or at worst, over white wine, never red.

Remember, too, that the correct word is "harvested," you know, like wheat, corn, soybeans, and such – the kinds of things sweaty, icky farmers from Flyover Land handle — and never off-putting, judgmental words like "dismembered" or "crushed." Ms. Manners reminds you that the only "sin" in liberalism is being judgmental.

Ms. Manners knows that you Enlightened Womyn of Today will be eating "clean," probably vegan, so there's little danger that talk about livers and limbs will remind you of any gross thing on your plate like a chicken leg or organ meats wrapped in bacon or anything, God forbid! You are much too sensitive for that! Your abiding and loud concern not only for whatever food paradigm is current this week, but for the well-being of the entire animal kingdom, not to mention the planet, goes without saying.

But Ms. Manners also knows that you are devoutly into recycling, religiously separating all manner of materials such as paper, glass and the evil plastic and aluminum. So, it would be a shame – would it not? – if you already have a variety of "parts" that could somehow be utilized and you failed to recycle? What if they could even be sold at a cost-plus profit in order to buy another pair of darling Jimmy Choo shoes? Some people take their aluminum cans to a recycling center themselves and make a little cashola. It's exactly the same thing. Pizza boxes, milk cartons, Pepsi cans, baby livers, same diff.

So, in conclusion, Ms. Manners suggests happy, cheery topics over your tofu, arugula and brown rice. A few starter ideas: making sure that testing cosmetics on animals is done with the highest regard for the health and safety of the dear wittle bitty animals; or saving rainforests, or banning paper and plastic bags. Fair Trade coffee, dolphin-free tuna – all fine topics Ms. Manners can endorse. Sales of baby livers harvested by experienced crushers that avoid mangling the liver is best saved for private quiet discussions far far from the prying eyes of guerrilla videographers and taxpayers bitching about being forced to pay for such atrocities simply because they hate womyn.

Bonus Discussion Question: How on Earth do you even find a heart, an arm, a liver in what we have been told for 42 years is "a clump of cells"? Good Lord! Is there a baby in there after all??

DISTINGUISHED MEMBERS

July 31, 2015

Please! I am begging here. In the name of all that's Holy, stop the fake rape charges! Honestly, I can't take it any more. I would love to write about something else. Anything else. Heck, maybe even guns and ammo again someday.

"But nooooooo....", as the late John Belushi used to say. Apparently, I am going to be forced to write about fake college rape cases forever. A new outrage comes to light every week. We women have been told for decades that we have "Penis Envy." And who could blame us? Look what those distinguished members can do!!

Father children. Urinate at a campout without even getting your socks wet. Write your name in the snow. Show a lady a good time. As they say on infomercials: "But wait, there's more!!"

At Amherst, a Magic Penis could assault a woman orally while its owner was unconscious! Whoa! Nothing tougher than escaping unwelcome attention from an unconscious man! This particular Magic Penis happened to belong to the boyfriend of the Fake Victim du Jour's roomie. The poor FVdJ evidently had somehow lost all her girlfriends when they learned she had betrayed her roommate. Awwww. She showed them! Twenty-one months – let that sink in! Twenty-one months! – after the "attack", (hers, as it happened) she charged the unconscious man (presumably, almost sobered up by then) with rape. And was believed. Because women never lie. Except for the legions who do.

Will there EVER be a consequence for these pathological liars, vindictive fabulists, and attention-seeking headcases? There should be jail time and serious financial repercussions for utterly ruining young men's lives. At least as serious as the 5 years in the clink and the quarter mil you will be fined for the unauthorized copying of a DVD.

I propose a year-long boycott – either total or selectively targeted – of sending our boys to college until the draconian, discriminatory rules governing normal courtship and kangaroo-court disciplinary procedures are rescinded. Oh, but only AFTER the boys have already been accepted. Just don't show up. Hit 'em where it hurts, in the wallet. Let them have a year of colleges half-filled with only hysterical ninnies. My dear Mother can tell you how fun college was when all the men left for war on December 8th, 1941. This IS a war and the lunatics are winning. Male Alumni and sane women alumnae should cease all donations.

What would it possibly hurt to have our boys sit out a year before college? Send the boys to trade school or the military for three years as the Israelis do. Let them work or travel. You can go a long way on the $65K it takes for a year at Male-Hating U. Better even they should just veg in Mom's basement reading Great Books. Not one penny to those evil, Stalinoid, freedom-loathing institutions until they take one giant step in the direction of sanity!

Evidently, the mere presence of a penis is enough to be Guilty of Something. Unless, and this is VERY important, unless that penis is attached to a person named Caitlyn. That is not a Magic Penis, or a Guilty Penis, but a mere decorative appendage which in no way indicates that Caitlyn is, in fact, a man. No, you hateful bigot. Caitlyn is a woman and the fact that she is still carrying a penis and accoutrements is of no more significance than if she were carrying a purse. Which she no doubt is, and probably a damn fine one with all the lucre rolling in. Furthermore, she always WAS a woman, Boy Howdy.

I'm told that one of the reasons the Mormons are so interested in genealogy is that if you convert, you can retroactively save all your dead relatives. Whatever. I've hardly ever met a Mormon I didn't like and admire personally; honestly, they seem to be wonderful people. I voted for one for President. Would that he had won. But I have to say that belief strikes me as a bit far-fetched. All due respect…scratch any religion, including my own, find a far-fetched belief or maybe even two.

But it's waaaay less far-fetched than the notion that that muscular guy on the Wheaties box, Best Male Athlete in the World, was actually a woman then, because he says he is one now. Even though he still has his package. Perhaps, if you want to nit-pick, it's a tad less robust than before due to an influx of estrogen sufficient to grow breasts, I can't say. Go to a baseball game on a warm day and you can see more impressive man-boobs even without estrogen. But those guys don't have reality shows and book deals and magazine covers and interviews worth millions and millions and millions of dollars.

We are at the Abyss, my friends. Our culture has one foot in the grave and the other on a banana peel. Throw in the nearly-unbelievable Rachel Dolezal case, and White is Black; Truth is Falsehood; Men are Women; and George Orwell was a cockeyed optimist.

DAYENU

August 7, 2015

As has been pointed out many, many times recently, when dozens of young Black men a week get killed by other Black men, it doesn't even make a ripple in the Black Lives Matter crowd. I once saw the following one-paragraph summation in the Chicago paper on about page 32: "A 16-year-old youth was killed Saturday night when he was stabbed in the head with a screwdriver by his friend in a fight over who would get to drive the car they had just stolen."(Screwdrivers kill. Clearly, they should be banned. Not for nothing is my house a Screwdriver-Free Zone.)

But let that same "16-year-old youth" (who could easily be 6'2" and 250 lbs.) get shot by a cop of a different color, pursuing the stolen car and it's "he only had a screwdriver and some Skittles!" So let's revisit the original incident where this year-long round of riots all began. I have a few additional thoughts on the Michael Brown disaster if you will bear with me. They are not amusing ones, I'm sorry to say. Some days there's just nothing funny to say, your mission as a Friday humorist, notwithstanding. Next week, I promise.

Near the end of the Passover Seder, the celebrants sing a song called "Dayenu" which means "It would have been enough." It goes on for roughly as long as I was in labor, (17 hours, in case it comes up on a quiz show) but the idea of it is a hymn of praise and thanks to the Almighty saying, "If you had just brought us out of Egypt" Dayenu. It would have been enough. "If you would have only parted the Red Sea," Dayenu. It would have been enough. "If you had only given us the Torah." Dayenu. You get the idea.

This song came unbidden to my mind as I thought about all the chances Michael Brown had to save his own life.

If he had only shot some buckets or played a video game instead of getting high and deciding that filching some smokes from a convenience store was a bright idea, he would be alive. At least until the next time he decided to commit a crime. Dayenu.

If The Gentle Giant had not decided as a parting shot to rough up the store clerk who was half his size. Maybe the clerk wouldn't even have called in the theft. What's a few cigars? Dayenu.

If, after stealing and assaulting, he had just walked away as unobtrusively as a 300-lb man can and not swaggered down the middle of the street, he would be alive today. If, when the officer approached him in his car, he had answered politely, and moved out of the street, he would be alive today. Dayenu.

If, when the officer approached him in his car and noticed that he fit the description of the shoplifter who assaulted the store clerk, he had said, "I'm sorry, officer, I was loaded and acted stupid. Here's the cigars and I want to apologize to the clerk," he would be alive today.

Almost certainly he would have been able to plead down the assault charge to 5th degree and if he returned the stolen merchandise, they would have let that go, too. "Justice" today is all about plea-bargaining. And several hundred "last chances."

If, once he made his decision to go after the cop, he had slugged him once and not grabbed at the gun, he would be in seriously deep do-do, but probably still alive. Now, he's got assaulting an officer to go with shoving the clerk and the petty theft, but Officer

Wilson was clearly no hothead. If Brown backs up, hands up, as the narrative pretends to go, and says, "I'm sorry; I'm sorry, that was stupid, I won't resist any further," he is probably alive.

If, after he grabs for the gun, it goes off, and he begins to run, he stops, turns, raises his hands and goes down to his knees or prone on the ground, waiting to be arrested, he might get roughed up a bit upon being "helped" into the squad car, but he is alive.

Even after he charges again and again and is shot multiple times, if he had stopped, gone to the ground with his hands locked behind his head, he is probably alive, headed for a hospital at taxpayer expense and then warehoused for a lot of his life, also at taxpayer expense. Apparently, it was the final head shot that killed him.

A senseless pointless crime. Cigars that could have been purchased for a few lousy dollars. Compounded by escalating stupidity of responses on Brown's part. A young man, with people who loved him, is dead. Another young man's life and career are in tatters. A town is in misery. Businesses are looted and burned. The social fabric is rent once again.

The forces of division and evil are doing their best to widen the rift from the highest reaches of political power to looting thugs – yes, thugs! – who just couldn't live without that can of purloined Pringles.

For awhile there, morons were invading brunch places and confronting white people who had nothing to do with Mr. Brown or any other dead criminal of any color. The plague spreads. To Baltimore. To Texas. Where next?

The ginned-up, sometimes hired, rage is stoked – for political gain, for jockeying for position, for profit in "Hands up" t-shirts; for fame on the talk shows; for a platform for Sharpton. To keep Black voters angry and mobilized. For professional race-baiters to write about as evidence of white people's endemic racism. Ah yes, my healing President, it's just in our DNA. Since you are half-white, how's that racist DNA going for you?

Dayenu.

CURMUDGEON GRRRLL

August 14, 2015

Even though I have been Ammo Grrrll for a couple of years now, for this week I am feeling a bit cranky and would like to be known as Curmudgeon Grrrll. And feelings – as we all know – are paramount. Especially for someone in a protected class of grievance-mongers, which, fortunately for me, includes women. In fact, call me Caitlyn Curmudgeon. Why not?

Curmudgeonery (getting wrapped around the axle about relatively minor things) is one of the sure signs you have passed from "late, late middle age" right into senior-ocity. Another sign is when you vigorously wave goodbye and slap yourself around with your triceps, but that's for another day. To the Curmudgeon, it feels like the last vestige of The Goode Olde Days is gone and nothing has changed for the better. Not a thing. Unless you count medical advances, flat-screen televisions, smart phones, ethnic food, UPS, central air-conditioning, email, The Internet in general, Skyping, stamps you stick instead of lick, cupholders in cars and movie theatres, or Amazon. Okay, a LOT of stuff is better, but I'm still feeling cranky.

I think when the epitaph of civilization is written, that it will be traced to the day that "party" became a verb instead of a noun. This really bugged me. A party was a nice event that used to involve either balloons, cake, ice cream, and presents, or much later, adult beverages in nice glasses, canapes, and pretty clothes. I loved parties.

Now when an idiot (def.: someone much younger than me, possibly more attractive, probably tattooed) says, "Woohoo! Let's party!" — or worse yet, "par-tay!" — he means, "Let's drink until we throw up. That sounds fun." Our son showed us a cable tv show in which people drank till they threw up, that's it, the whole show, another sign of the Apocalypse.

And what's up with all the woo-hooing, too? When did that start? An artist starts to sing a song in a live concert and the audience members scream to indicate "I recognize that song!" A television camera is turned on a crowd at a sporting event and right on cue, everyone screams. Am I the only one that finds this odd? Makes you long for the dignified guy quietly holding up the John 3:16 sign.

I don't know which came first, but in addition to party becoming a verb, the words "evil" or "just plain wrong" also became replaced with the weasel word "inappropriate." Long ago an acquaintance of mine got roaring drunk at a corporate gathering (she could have been on that cable show) and started throwing her food around. She was a Diversity hire, so she was not (yet) fired for this, but was counseled for "inappropriate" behavior. And, as usual, my tendency to blurt out what I think did not endear me to this (former) acquaintance. "Good Heavens, Brunhilde (not her real name). Did your supervisor happen to mention in what circumstances food-throwing would actually be 'appropriate'? Because I would be curious."

Calling something "wrong" is so yesterday, so judgmental. And down the slippery slope we have slid. I always think we may be at the bottom where we could find purchase to push off and lift ourselves up a bit; but there is no bottom.

My last peeve, may, indeed, be called my Pet Peeve. Anyone, stranger or friend, in my vicinity will be made aware of this peeve when the occasion arises. He will notice a small, severely-agitated woman hopping about like Rumpelstiltskin and using what the movie rating people call "Language." And that is people who are too lazy and irresponsible to return their shopping carts to a cart corral. To me, this is another sign of The End of the World As We Know It.

I swear on everything I hold dear that most carts abandoned willy-nilly in the parking lot are no more than 20 feet from the nearest corral. In many cases, closer than that. I once watched a very nicely-dressed woman in an Escalade strap her baby into its carseat and then leave the cart right there when, if she had taken it with her, there was a corral right next to the driver's side door!! And even though the Jewish texts speak of all 613 commandments as having equal weight, I recognize that shooting someone, even in Arizona, is not an equivalent offense to cart abandonment. Plus I cannot locate the precise prohibition against Cart Abandonment in even the shadow of the penumbra of the Torah.

And let's stipulate that it is Arizona. It's very, very, very hot and you want to get back in an air-conditioned vehicle as quickly as possible. The asphalt is hot. The handle on the cart is hot. That is still no excuse to dump it in a Handicapped spot, for sure. Nor is it sporting to abandon yours in the only empty stall with some pitiful shade from a random twig, rendering that stall unusable without the next person having to get out of her vehicle and move the cart.

So, what, my friends, is your opinion on what is going on here? Simple laziness? Is it that a terrifying proportion of our fellow Americans are too fat and unfit to walk 20 feet? (Too much Golden Corral to walk to the cart corral?) Is it that we have a substantial coddled group of entitled people that think "Aw, someone else will pick up after me. They always have."? Does the massive political corruption teach everyone it's okay not to follow rules (see, Sanctuary City, illegal immigration, Solyndra and much more)?

Please put your cart in a corral. The stroke you prevent may save a beloved (or perhaps just a beliked) humor columnist. Thank you. And have a lovely weekend. I'm considerably less cranky after venting. Mr. Ammo Grrrll thanks you, too. He is dialing even as we speak to cancel his reservation at the Motel 6. They'll have to leave the light on for somebody else.

CUSTOMER SERVICE

August 21, 2015

So, I'm sitting at home in my Dusty Little Village after having returned from shooting in a nearby Dusty Bigger Village. I got a new Sig Sauer .45 with almost no kick. Just chillin' and enjoying an adult beverage as dinner was bubbling happily away in the oven, not feeling at all like Cranky Caitlyn the Curmudgeon Grrrll, when my cellphone rings with a blocked number.

Now, first of all, the cellphone is supposedly on a "Don't Call" List. Which works as well as one-size-fits-all panty hose. Then, the caller calls me by my given name which, it may surprise you to know, is not Ammo. "Susan?" he asks. Like we're buddies. So that was his first mistake. The second mistake was announcing that this was a "courtesy" call to tell me that my business had been approved for a $250,000 loan. Color me surprised! Not only did I not apply for a loan, even for $2.50, but more curiously, I do not have a business. "Hmm...this must be a definition of 'courtesy' with which I am not familiar," I said before disconnecting. I miss the ability to slam down the receiver. Whatever the scam was, it must work or they wouldn't do it.

However, for balance in all things, I must report that the other night out to dinner Mr. Ammo Grrrll and I had a very pleasant customer service experience.

The Ak-Chin Casino has a lovely upscale restaurant called The Range which features excellent food and even better service. When we asked for some minor item to be brought to our table (probably more butter if I know me), the server actually said, "My pleasure." It was her pleasure to serve us, imagine that!! Most of the time young servers, who are clearly trying to be accommodating in their fashion, say "No problem" when presented with a minor request. Now I really hate to sound like a jerk, but here's the thing: when I ask you to do the job I am paying for, I want you to do the little task I have requested even if it IS a "problem."

"My pleasure" just sounds so much better. The server was not a young person. And, our appreciation was expressed robustly in the traditional manner.

The worst customer service event of my life happened to me in New Jersey. I had been hired by New Jersey Gas and Electric Company to entertain at a big company event. I flew in from our wintering rental condo on a hellacious flight in a snowstorm. The employee sent to pick me up from the airport had been assigned a company car in which the last person driving it had clearly not had a shower in a long long time and was on Day Six of his Five-Day-Deodorant Pad. My escort was mortified.

She dropped me off at my Hilton and promised to have a different car in which to fetch me for the event. After inhaling at last, I got in a long line for check-in. The woman on duty had big hair, bubble gum, and a sour look that conveyed "I hate my job in general and you in particular." She found my reservation and asked, "How were you planning to pay for this?"

"Oh," I replied, smiling and handing her the embossed stationery my client had sent me in advance. "Here's the letter from New Jersey Gas & Electric asking you to bill it to their account. That number right there."

And SHE said: "Anyone could write this letter."

It takes quite a lot to render me speechless, but I was too

flummoxed for a minute to utter a word. And then I said, "Here's my VISA. Please just charge it to that until we get this straightened out, but are you calling me a liar in front of all these people? And are you suggesting that if I were a scam artist trying to cadge one night's free hotel room out of someone in February that I would fly from San Diego to NEWARK???"

Miss Congeniality continued to chew gum, radiating hate for all humanity, and the line behind me exuded extreme annoyance with ME (The Lying Con Artist) for holding up the line, rather than any kind of support. I have pretty much stayed out of New Jersey since.

Balance in all things once again: In Columbus, MS, speaking at a women's college there, I had the morning free to go for a walk around the lovely town. I stopped in to a local coffee emporium, got coffee and asked for bottled water to go. The young lady at the counter was not particularly welcoming, a little curt, nothing terrible, as she informed me they didn't have bottled water. And a gentleman two people behind me in line, ran down the street after me and said, "I did not care for the way she spoke to you and I mean to tell her mother when I see her in church. Heavens, what must you think of our town! Please come over to my clothing store. We keep bottled water in our break room."

He introduced me to all his salesclerks, two black ladies and two white ladies, gave me the water he promised me and sent me on my way, "old friends who've just met" (to quote a Muppet lyric). OK, after selling me a skirt, a sweater, and a blouse, but still…

I was a Yankee raised to be terrified of The South. But I love its friendliness and charm. And also the fact that black and white people know each other as people. For another thing, you can get grits for breakfast in the South. In the Deep South, I was happily surprised to find that you get grits whether you order them or not. And what has surprised YOU, friends, good and bad, in the realm of customer service?

Update to readers, as I edit this for Volume 2, in early December, 2018:

I got a LOT of flak from people younger than geezers about my preference for "My pleasure" over "No problem." Now, I did not in any way suggest that I thought that phrase deserved punishment in the form of a bad tip; all I said was that I preferred it. I consider myself to be a very good tipper – our son was a waiter/busboy back in the day – and, in fact, will not even go out for a meal with someone who I know to be a bad tipper.

Nevertheless, the comments in the comment section felt that I was being an old-fashioned, crabby, old crone. I will stipulate to that and apologize abjectly for any waitperson I may have offended. Even though it didn't affect your tip.

WHO IS WISE?

August 8, 2015

The ancient Jewish text, the Talmud, asks, "Who is wise?" and answers, "Who learns from everyone." (As a topic for a future discussion, it also asks, "Who is rich?" and answers, "Who is satisfied with what he has." Is that a laugh riot, or what? We can't have THAT in the socialist paradise of Cherokee Lizzie, Class-Envy Bernie and Disparate Impact Barry, now can we?)

But, back to the notion that everyone has some wisdom to impart. Apparently, in the Olden Days, "credentials" were not as important as they are now. So, Sarah Palin would not have been mocked for taking awhile to graduate from an aggregate of colleges, not one of which was Harvard or Yale. Boise? I mean, is that even a thing? It must be in Utah or Montana or some other redneck Western state full of armed white guys clinging to God and guns. And Scott Walker would not have been ridiculed for failing to finish college either. Bill Gates, fellow drop-out, gets a pass; he's a liberal and a billionaire, so he can say, "Bite me."

So, wisdom comes from a variety of sources according to the ancient texts.

Case in point: A friend of mine learned something from a pimp.

This particular pimp just had a small stable of girls, a part-time job really. Unusually ambitious for someone in the pimping profession, he wisely kept another lucrative job on a union automobile assembly line as well, which is where my friend met him. Guess pimping doesn't usually include double overtime and dental insurance. Anyway, he gave my friend the following advice which stuck with me forever. Even though I was not present at the conversation, I'm going to put his words in quotes to clarify who was speaking. That may not be kosher stylistically according to the Journalist's Handbook, but there are no journalists any more anyway, so deal with it. My friend recalled the conversation very vividly.

"Marc," he said to my friend, "Only a lowlife, ignorant pimp needs to beat his girls. The smart pimp knows how to control his women with words. What I do, see, if the girl is beautiful, is pick at her, and belittle her and destroy her confidence. I point out all her flaws and make her so unsure of herself that she is dependent on me for her self-esteem, which I dole out with an eye-dropper."

"With an average or kinda fat, ugly girl, I do just the opposite. I tell her she's beautiful and build her up and again, she is dependent on me for her self-esteem. She'll do anything for me to get confirmation that she's a fox and not what she sees in the mirror."

I got to thinking about the Left and how they operate in exactly the same way. If you have bothered to pay attention in school, work hard, accumulate some savings, avoid drug or alcohol dependence, not been a criminal, possibly even been married to the mother or father of your children, the Alinsky-schooled Leftist belittles your success with "You didn't build that!" Hell, it's only your "White Skin Privilege" that got you ahead! (If you do not have white skin, then any success is because you are an Uncle Tom, Aunt Jemima, etc....see, Condi Rice, Justice Thomas, Ted Cruz, Marco Rubio, Dr. Ben Carson, Mia Love, the list goes on including many non-famous achievers. Surprisingly, the non-famous are people, too.)

I believe one of the reasons that the super-rich, especially of inherited wealth, are so often leftist is because they REALIZE that they have not earned their wealth. That it is just a result of the "lottery" Dear Leader speaks of. And he should know.

On the other hand, if you have not done one thing right in your life – if you have made one disastrous life decision after another – and someone assures you that you are still "beautiful," that nothing that has happened to you has ever been your fault because the system is stacked against you, then you will follow that leader to the ends of the earth.

Rush Limbaugh has a running theme that asserts that we never get out of high school. That the nerds and outcasts among us still long to sit with the Cool Kids in the Lunchroom. The former fat kid who is now an important, if portly, governor still dissolves into happy tears from a phone call from Bruce Springsteen.

It is a powerful form of social control. And, like the clever pimp, the government doesn't even need to "beat" people to exert that control. Why, play your cards right and you, too, could get invited to Gwyneth's mansion to have your picture taken with Dear Leader! Not that the Beating Option is off the table entirely, of course, as Lois Lerner or the Cake Bullies can attest. All political power is ultimately backed up by brutal force. Brow-beat and harass nuns for objecting to paying for abortifacients? Just another day at the office.

But granting access to the "VIP Room of Life," being the arbiters of Cool, the gatekeepers guarding the trends, the fads, the politically-correct speech code, is less trouble and less dangerous than facing down angry mobs. Sometimes, "in the course of human events" and all that, angry mobs – even nuns! – can be pushed far enough to fight back. And decide for themselves what is Cool. May the time not be distant.

GREAT EXPECTATIONS

September 4, 2015

I reckon I was about three when I had one of the biggest disappointments of my young life. We were at a carnival of some kind and, after enduring sustained, relentless wheedling, Daddy bought me some cotton candy. Whipped pink sugar on a stick – what could be better? Most anything, as it turned out.

All that promising pretty froth and you put a wad in your mouth and it melts away to nothing. It could almost be a metaphor for the huge, frothy 2014 Republican victory, but I don't want to talk about politics today. Especially since that Republican majority is slaving around the clock, building the fence to protect our border, reducing the debt, repealing and replacing Obamacare, scuttling the disastrous Iran deal, and reforming the tax code, so…say what? They aren't? Seriously? Nada, bupkiss, nuthin'? Not even the Iran deal?

Well, crap, there's ANOTHER big disappointment. Also, I hear there's no Santa Claus, but you couldn't prove it by the last several Administrations.

I spent 30 years on the road in my comedy career, living out of a suitcase and staying in hotels that escalated nicely in quality over those decades. Early on, two other comics and I once stayed in a motel outside Omaha whose motto probably was, "You can't see our parking lot from the highway!" A room cost $14.00 a "night" and the clerk was befuddled by guests who intended not only to stay the WHOLE night, but for three fun-filled days.

I have always enjoyed hotels. Until my sister — the fanatic germophobe — gave me a synopsis of some buzz-killing exposé she had watched which asserted that one might as well immerse in a vat of bacteria as touch anything in a hotel room. Particularly the remote control, light switches, bedspread, or shower. Thanks, Sis. Purell should give you freebies for life.

Though my clients often put me in five-star Marriotts, Ritz Carltons, and the like, as I enjoyed John Hinderaker's recent English travelogue with accompanying pictures, it seemed to me that he stayed in rather nicer hotels than I am accustomed to. For example, I'm going to guess that never once did his hotelier have a Post-It Note affixed to his headboard advertising that they had troubled themselves to provide clean linens. John? Yes, truly, in my last Hampton Inn in Texas there was a yellow Post-It note printed to look written with a Sharpie that boasted "SHEETS ARE CLEAN FOR YOUR ARRIVAL." Hosanna! They were so proud it made me wonder whether this was a recent departure from previous practices.

"Clean sheets? You betcha! Not so much in the past, but now we have decided to provide them. And we're just pleased as punch, so we want to bring this to your attention via this attractive, if somewhat scary, note."

Aren't clean sheets pretty much the most minimal standard for a hotel room, a normal expectation? Periodically one of my foster kids who was (and undoubtedly still is) a pathological liar would come to me and declare that he had decided to stop lying. His tone and demeanor were always one of believing that he deserved some kind of special credit for this resolution. And I would have to explain to him that, no, you do not get gold stars for not lying. Telling the truth is a standard expectation. It is a basic starting point for being a trustworthy, standup kind of guy. And I also explained to him that, although he had had a hard life, one of the reasons he did not trust anyone was because he himself could not be trusted.

Another of the saddest falls from great expectations for me has been the utter degeneration of the feminist movement and the whiny, hateful, wussie-pants quality of today's female grievance-mongers. Ladies, you are a flat-out embarrassment.

When I marched for equal opportunity in the '60s and '70s, I honestly believed that women would just get tougher and more competent and confident.

And clearly, we have paved the way for two or three wonderful levies of brilliant, talented, kick-ass young women – Michelle Malkin, Eliana Johnson, Heather Mac Donald, Mollie Hemingway, Mary Katherine Ham, to name but a few. Those, of course, are writers. There are also millions of doctors, dentists, lawyers, astronauts, CEOs and athletes. My great expectations were that once barriers were down, women would soar. And millions have.

It never occurred to me that we were simultaneously breeding a crop of spoiled, furious, entitled, intolerant loons who needed Trigger Warnings and Safe Rooms to retreat to in the unlikely event that anyone dared to disagree with them. That their delicate ears could not handle hearing things that upset them. Which was most everything. That ordinary courtship rituals and mutually-pleasurable sex would be defined as rape at the whim of vindictive headcases. Or, frankly, that standards would be lowered substantially to accommodate them. I expected that if women became firefighters or Marines, it would be because we had made the grade and exceeded it, not that the goalposts had been moved.

Oh, well. They say that a cynic is just a disappointed

idealist. *Great expectations.* It's still my favorite book by Charles Dickens.

THE THRIFTY MAMA

September 11, 2015

A few weeks ago, this column featured our next-door neighbor, not for nothing called The Thrifty Texan. Oh, he's good. Real good. But a profligate next to my Thrifty Mama. She wrote the book on thrift. (I once told Mr. Ammo Grrrll that "my middle name is 'thrift'," and he said, "Yes, but, unfortunately, your first name is 'Spend.'" He can be quite the card, that guy.)

We have also previously discussed Mama's growing up in the Dust Bowl in South Dakota during the Depression. Her family were sharecroppers when grasshoppers, Russian thistles, and drought destroyed what crops there were to share. Though Daddy made a fine living throughout their marriage, she just never got over being that poor as a kid. You can take the girl out of the Depression, but it's hard to take the Depression out of the girl.

We knew to warn any friends eating over to watch the condiments for "thinning." Any ketchup or mustard left in the bottom of a bottle would be swished with water to get the last drops. The unsuspecting could find their burger swimming in Lake Ketchup. We had many an exotic concoction of jellies and jams as she would combine dribs and drabs from several jars. "Anyone for Strawberry-Blueberry-Apricot-Orange Marmalade?"

She always bought chickens whole and cut them up herself which probably saved well over a dime a pound. As a young bride, I tried to emulate her thrift; however, I was both lazy and incompetent, a deadly combo. I learned early on that I was not going to be a surgeon. There was never a recognizable piece of the bird and for some reason, Mr. Ammo Grrrll found it important to know whether he was eating a leg or a wing.

Mother considered buying orange juice not from concentrate to be the highest form of waste. She was and is unfailingly kind to everyone, but the ladies in the neighborhood who bought cartons of pre-made juice would be spoken of in hushed but disapproving tones. We always had a juice pitcher and the kids would take turns being tasked with stirring the frozen orange mush into juice. She would sneak in an extra half can of water, too, to extend it further.

When I went to Northwestern – the first time I had been away from home for longer than a week – I longed for the simple food of home. Casseroles (called Hot Dish in Minnesota, of course), such as Tuna Hot Dish with Peas and a gooey crust of crushed Potato Chips. Or Chipped Beef in Cream Soups on Chow Mein Noodles, a dish which must have had 5,000 mgs of sodium per bite. We never had a cut of meat that didn't have to be braised for 4-5 hours to get tender. My first meal at Northwestern, they served something called "Roast Beef Au Jus" which I believed was going to be my familiar Pot Roast, but which was a thin, rare piece of pathetic meat you could see through, sitting in the "au jus" which turned out to be, well, blood. Oh dear.

One day, long after I was a successful comedian, we stopped in to a shopping complex on the river and found a fancy truffle shop – chocolates, not the kind French pigs root around for. I asked her to pick out four truffles to be placed in a pretty little box to be eaten later. (The chocolates, not the box...) She kept asking how much they were and I kept assuring her that it didn't matter. Reluctantly, she picked out four and the saleslady boxed them and tied a bow around them. The lady said, "Five dollars, please," which I considered quite reasonable. Mother screamed. Literally. And told the startled saleswoman to put them back.

I said, "Mother, some things are just worth it. Now stop making a scene and let's go sit on that park bench and eat one." She nibbled at one but couldn't even enjoy it thinking about the extravagance of a piece of candy that cost $1.25 when the rent on their farmhouse had been $8.00 a month. (One of their best friends, who had grown up equally poor but was now a millionaire South Dakota farmer, also refused on principle to pay $2.00 for a hot dog at the Twins game. Clearly, that price was some time ago. Now, he'd need a defibrillator.)

However, one thrift measure was a bridge too far even for her. We had bought an old chest freezer from a co-worker. On one visit, Mother decided she would clean out this freezer. And oh, the things she found! One was a broken package of meatballs, three years past its sell-by date, with the meatballs spilling out unprotected onto the bottom of the freezer. She threw the meatballs out onto the grass in the backyard hoping some scavenger would find them.

And indeed he did. My neighbor, Thriftiest-of-All Randy, suddenly single and also unemployed, and cooking for three adolescent children, saw her do it, scooped them up, picked the grass off, put them in spaghetti sauce and fed them to his children for dinner. With Taco Bell napkins. Beat that. Happily, everyone survived.

WHEN YOU MUST GO HOME AGAIN

September 18, 2015

Thomas Wolfe notwithstanding, sometimes one must go home again. On August 18, the little Thrifty Mama we discussed last week – 94-and-a-half and one of few residents in her Assisted Living facility not using a walker – decided to compete in the tumbling portion of the Olympics, Late, Late Senior Division. The corrupt French judge gave her only a "2" for not sticking the landing.

Okay, what actually happened of course, is that she experienced a bout of extreme vertigo from a nasty combo of inner ear issues and a sudden blood pressure drop and she fell. By the grace of God, this teeny little woman, who looks like she would break every bone in her body if she sat down hard, did not even fracture a bone. Milk at every meal, people! But she did sustain a brain bleed, an ugly eleven-inch laceration on her arm, and most impressive bruising. Her teeny arms looked like two long, thin eggplants.

I was called by the local ER and told that nothing could be done for her but "comfort care." There's a lovely way to start your day. My brother, the nurse, hightailed it from the Twin Cities up to St. Cloud where he had had her moved to avail us of neurosurgery services. The words, "Screw 'comfort'!" may have been spoken. Fortunately, the bleed was "small" – ah, what a lovely word! – surgery was not necessary, and she was released in a few days, battered and confused, but very much alive. Feisty, even.

Meanwhile, I had cancelled a raft of appointments, sent Scott four columns, loaded up the car and had begun driving once again from Arizona to Minnesota. It isn't nearly as fun when you are on a strict schedule as when you can meander and just enjoy the trip. And when you feel you must take a black dress and high heels just in case. Strangers of every race and color along the way encouraged me and told me they would be praying. Lord, I love this country!

I was able to stay for 15 days, cooking and caretaking. Daddy had mensched up pretty well at trying to do a few basic household tasks but was more than thrilled to turn those duties over to me. It is amazing how quickly the role reversal takes hold. A Mother who used to feed a picky toddler by saying, "Here comes the dumptruck," now eats like a bird. Since child-rearing is a careful balance of threats and bribes, I offered to buy her all new clothes if she could get over 100 lbs. (Safe offer. Not gonna happen...) and threatened to go back to Arizona (RIGHT NOW!) if she didn't eat ONE blueberry pancake! You gotta do what you gotta do. She ate. Two, even. And part of a third.

Mother attained a kind of celebrity. It is a sad fact that death is a constant companion in most assisted living facilities and nursing homes. You make a new friend; she dies a few months later. Someone goes away to the hospital and never returns. Mother's return was tantamount to having that dog your mother said "went to a nice farm" come loping back down the street. Other residents surrounded her in awe, coming close to touching the hem of her garment.

So now she has a walker. She and Daddy do a hilarious version of Bumper Cars with the two walkers in their smallish apartment. You should see them when the phone rings. Even though it is a cordless phone, Heaven forfend you should take the phone to where you are. A phone belongs in a stationary position as God intended, and so that is where it will stay. Just get used to talking over the answering machine which comes on after the maximum number of rings.

Medicare does do an excellent job with rehab services for injured seniors. Sure it's unsustainable, but for now it was a lifesaver. Being a lifelong Republican somewhere to the right of Ted Cruz, Mother feels guilty for even using these services and conspired to shuck them as quickly as she could. She refused Occupational Therapy for her hand. Classic take: "What do I need with an occupation at my age?"

Her laceration healed nicely as well and she is afraid she won't even get a good scar out of it for sympathy and a conversation piece. I told her they probably sell fake scars at Spencers around Hallowe'en and that cheered her.

We dodged the bullet this time. We were able to have wonderful family time for Daddy's 90th birthday which fell a couple weeks after the accident. Darn few people my age (late, late middle age, as you recall) still have two living parents. You rejoice, one day at a time, the way we all know we should live, even while keeping the black dress in the front of the closet. For those of you less lucky, my deepest sympathies, no matter how long it's been.

WHY I LOVE COUNTRY MUSIC

September 25, 2015

There is a biopic about the eccentric jazz genius Thelonius Monk called "Straight, No Chaser." I saw it years ago. In one scene that made a vivid impression on me, some snotty, self-absorbed "journalist" whose name I didn't catch – who cares? — is interviewing Mr. Monk and asks him what kind of music he likes. Monk says, "I like ALL music." And with sarcasm dripping from his voice into a puddle on the floor, the man then asks what he thinks is a clever "gotcha" question: "Do you like COUNTRY music?" And Monk says to the camera, "The man must have a hearin' problem."

This can't be! The hippest-ever black jazz pianist can't possibly enjoy a genre of music favored by white rednecks who cling to God and guns and marry their cousins!

The world works so much better for the intolerant when they can put people into neat bins. That's why a conservative black man or the happy heterosexual woman who doesn't hate men drives the culture warriors out of what passes for their minds.

There are several reasons why I love country music. Originally, I thought I would buttress my arguments quoting hundreds of great lyrics, but I didn't know what copyright rules I might be infringing upon and also the column would end up the size of a major piece of legislation, only without lies, pork or bridges to nowhere. So, this will not be a comprehensive analysis, just my humble opinion. You are (still, so far) free to hold your own opinion, even though if you don't like country music, you are wrong. And possibly evil. Haha, I kid.

First of all, almost all of the country artists can actually sing and play their own instruments. When you have a band like Willie Nelson's or Mel Tillis's — musicians who have been together for much longer than any of them have been with any number of successive wives — you can be assured that the band will be tighter than a wet wool sweater accidentally thrown in a clothes dryer on the "Cotton Hot" setting.

From the angelic purity of Patsy Cline's voice to the beautiful four-part harmonies of Little Big Town, with few exceptions, you're in for just plain good music.

Secondly, most country music is ABOUT something. Something important. Long-term marriage, infidelity, love won, love lost, children, messing up bad enough to warrant jail, redemption, love for mama, overcoming obstacles.

Sure, there have also been a boatload of drinking songs, cheatin' songs, and plain ol' feel-good tunes about raising Cain. I'm going to stipulate that "Red Solo Cup" may not be fraught with nuance. I still like it and it's an excellent tool to ensure solitude as Mr. Ammo Grrrll can't stand it.

Country music is also a paean to "ordinary" people, whether it's George Strait's "Brothers of the Highway" about truckers, or the popular theme that a man makes a mistake who marries for money when he can get better lovin' from a down-home country girl. (Toby Keith's "I Like Girls Who Drink Beer," to name but one.)

As a writer and comedian, I have a particular fondness for songs with clever lyrics. Brad Paisley is exceptionally adept at these, but clever lyricists abound in the genre. In a cultural and artistic desert of anti-American sentiment, here is an oasis of unembarrassed love of God and country.

There is also an appreciation of unabashed masculinity that is refreshing. Daddies are a positive force in the lives of their children, imagine that! The yin and yang of the male and the female are noted and celebrated. For both wit and truth, check out Brad Paisley's "You Need A Man Around Here." Or his "Ode de Toilet" about the great battle over the position of the toilet seat in the war of the sexes. And, of course, the age-old conundrum of how to convince a woman to go to bed: Toby Keith's "A Little Less Talk…Little More Action" or his hilarious (with surprise ending) "Get Out of Your Clothes, or Get Out of My Car."

Now, having tried to persuade the unconvinced that country music is grand, let me also say that there is no reason to confine oneself to a single genre, any more than a steady diet of just steak and taters will satisfy forever. Try the halibut, at least once, for Pete's sake! Maybe tofu, even. I'm on a current campaign to get our neighbor, the Paranoid Texan, to join us at a symphony. It's going about as well as Hillary's campaign. Maybe if I put on a robotic smile?

What has long bewildered and depressed me is why everything has to be "either-or." How quick we humans are to form mutually-exclusive tribal loyalties. If you love cats, you must hate dogs. If you watch NASCAR, you are duty-bound to hate soccer. Why?

I love Mozart, Brahms, Rachmaninoff, and Gershwin. I love French accordion music, Mexican mariachi bands, the Eagles, the Beatles, Sinatra and Ella Fitzgerald. I enjoy live jazz, and nearly faint at Pavarotti's rendition of the aria Nessun Dorma. Does this wide-ranging taste make me some sort of superior elevated soul? Probably. Haha, again with the kidding. No, seriously, I just ask, "In a harsh and difficult world, why deliberately cheat yourself out of any form of beauty?"

Several operatic arias will wring emotion from me. But they've got nothing on country music. The first few lines of Cal Smith's "Hello, Country Bumpkin" will bring a lump to my throat and by the end, I will be bawling like a baby.

OCTOBER, NOVEMBER and DECEMBER

The fall columns of 2015 begin with -- once again into the breech -- attacking the worst of Politically Correct Group Think with a column called "Weasel Words". And the one that follows will relate a few rather hilarious times when random busybodies assumed "racism" not in evidence.

I am rather proud of the October 30th column called "Tiptoeing" which deals with one of my core beliefs – and that is that we pamper our kids today at their own peril. Not only are we doing our society a great disservice by producing a crop of fragile whiners who are terrified of disagreement or independent thought, but we are creating a generation with no more resilience and "fight" than a sick person whose immune system is completely shot. It cannot end well.

In a column near the 52nd anniversary of the assassination of President Kennedy – can that be possible? And yet everyone around my age and older can remember exactly where they were when they heard about it – you will find a column on how far the Democrat Party has moved left from the ideals of the late President. His stirring words "Ask not what your country can do for you, but what you can do for your country," could not even be uttered today without being attacked as racist, sexist, and any other deplorable "ist" that could be thought up. The over-arching theme of today's Democrat Party is, "You are an entitled victim. Somebody, somewhere owes you money. Not only should you not do anything FOR your country, but the very concept of a country with borders is racist."

As we head into the late winter and early spring batch of columns, and the year turns to 2016, there will be a full-throated wish for one and all to have a Merry Christmas!

WEASEL WORDS

October 2, 2015

Any living language can mutate. A friend in college said he had studied some kind of High German for reading philosophy. When he tried to use that language conversationally in a visit to Germany, he learned he was speaking the equivalent of English from Chaucer. "Prithee canst thou tell me, sire, where might be the street which returneth me to my hostel?" he might say. People either backed away from a potential lunatic or laughed in his face. So, language and the meaning of language evolve. I get that.

Nevertheless, it is disheartening in the extreme to see how many words and phrases – when uttered by The Perpetually Aggrieved SJWs – have come to mean "I cannot and will not tolerate disagreement. Daddy Government says I don't have to." Let us examine but three.

COMFORTABLE – It started a few decades ago with the seemingly-innocuous "comfortable."

Bonus joke: A little old Jewish guy in Brooklyn is bicycling and hit by a car. Though not seriously injured, as a precaution he is immobilized by the EMTs, one of whom asks, "Are you comfortable?" And the little guy says, "I do all right."

So "comfortable" has come to mean not only curled up in a Barcalounger, but an alternative meaning is being well-off enough to afford a pleasant lifestyle, but not rich-rich.

One day, having lunch in Minnesota with a woman friend, I said something positive about President Bush and my friend said, "That makes me uncomfortable." It caught me off guard. I wanted to ask, "What? Your pantyhose are chafing? You're in a draft? What in the world are you talking about and who told you you were guaranteed a life of eternal comfort? Why don't you just say you disagree? I can handle it." But, of course, I said nothing. I just moved to Arizona. Here we are only "uncomfortable" when it's over 115.

VIOLENCE – Talk to any SJW for any length of time and you learn that everything is "violence." Swearing. Shouting. Pointing. Disagreement in particular. Years after I (finally) got a degree from a Minnesota State College, I went into their Administration Building and saw little plaques on all the desks that bragged, "This is a violence-free workplace." Well, glory be, that would distinguish it from all the other workplaces where fisticuffs and gunplay are a normal part of the day. Seriously? Was there a big problem with Assault and Battery before you hit on the obvious solution of putting up plaques?

What is the real message here? Nobody is allowed to disagree sharply. And here we have not only a male-female divide, but a yuge class divide. I have worked blue collar jobs with men for most of my working life. In my night-shift print shop job (80 men and me), disagreements occasionally resulted in some pushing and shoving, and very rarely, in a couple of punches being thrown. If the bosses or foremen came around, "nobody saw nuthin." It was settled, as the saying goes, "like men." Nobody ever got seriously injured and nobody would have called it "violence." It was "blowing off steam" plus a perfectly-rational way for grown men to settle important questions such as which Charlie's Angel was the hottest.

When I hear a Pajama Boy say that strong disagreement, even angry speech, is "violence," I just want one of those cartoon boxing gloves on a spring to come out of nowhere and punch him in the head: "See? Now, granted, that WAS violence. Before we were just talking. Feel the difference?" OK, I lied. I want to do it myself. I know it's wrong; it's not enlightened, it's not kind; it's not feminine; and it's definitely not Jewish. I recently fasted for 25 hours to atone for thoughts like this. But that's how strongly I feel about equating mere speech with assault.

SAFE – When I hear the word "safe," I picture Jackie Robinson stealing home. Or I think of a heavy metal box in which you put the guns not in your vehicles or on your person. It does not mean "perpetual freedom from encountering challenging or controversial ideas."

Oh, Lord, help us. Now we have "safe rooms" with Play-Doh and plush toys to provide succor to embarrassing whine-babies who must be protected from all views that don't conform to the crap they have been spoon-fed from nursery school to college.

As soon as someone claims to be "offended" or worse yet, to "feel unsafe," the discussion is automatically over. It's really a nasty, intellectually-dishonest tactic to change the subject completely. You're losing, so let's not make it about the subject under discussion, but about your feelings.

Since there is no "right or wrong" with feelings and everybody is entitled to as many feelings as she can generate, then the moral high ground is already ceded. And the person who disagreed with her and made her feel "unsafe" is clearly a vicious "bully."

It is way past time to call people on this. The next person who says "I don't feel safe," or "I am offended," should be told, "Who cares? Grow up." Sure, you'll lose your job, be branded a sexist, racist homophobe and end up a social pariah, but this murder of language must end. Our freedom depends on it. You go first.

The very thought makes me feel uncomfortable and unsafe. "Honey, can you bring me the Play-Doh and my Pooh Bear?"

ASSUMPTIONS

October 9, 2015

I remember an outstanding episode of *The Odd Couple* in which Felix ended up in court over some minor incident. Naturally, he acted as his own attorney. When a hostile witness used the word "assume," he pounced. "Aha! When you 'assume,' you make an 'ass' of 'u' and 'me,'" he said triumphantly.

And nowhere can one go further wrong, or make a bigger "ass" of "u" and "me" than in the complex realm of "racism," real or imagined. I offer but three examples.

Many years ago, I was in a restaurant with my best friend enjoying a hamburger in a tall booth. The subject of my weekly housekeeper came up and – not for the first time – I said, "I really have to find a way to let her go. She has no common sense. She shows up late or not at all and never the same day of the week. She wants to spend the first hour of her time telling me her problems. She hangs her coat in the back hall and it reeks of cigarette smoke which permeates the whole house. And she is so relentlessly depressed that she brings me down for days. But she needs the job. What can I do?"

To leap ahead in the story just a bit, she solved my problem by quitting on her own without notice not too long after that. But, as it happened, our conversation was being eavesdropped upon by a thin blonde busybody in an adjacent booth. She got up, looked daggers at me, and said, "I heard what you said about your cleaning woman and I think you should be ashamed of yourself for your racism."

Stunned, I could only say, "I'm sorry you had to overhear that. It may have sounded kind of mean. But my cleaning woman is as white as the driven snow. My own mother is a cleaning woman. Do you think that all cleaning women are black or that all black women are cleaning women?"

She opened her mouth several times like a baby bird and then shut it again and (slinked? slank?) slunk out.

The second incident happened in the early '80s in Macon, Georgia. It was my first time in the South, other than making a connecting flight in either Memphis or Atlanta.

The event at which I was entertaining wasn't until evening. I got up fairly early to go for a walk in the lovely town, which still had a functioning downtown. I could smell some kind of awesome flowers, jasmine and possibly magnolias. I wandered for several blocks enjoying the beautiful homes and feel of the place.

And then, like a movie unfolding, I saw trouble up ahead. Imagine two perpendicular streets coming together to form a corner. Down one side came two young white men wearing feed caps, jeans, and t-shirts. They were muscular guys, laughing and punching each other in the shoulder as they joked around. Bubbas! Rednecks! Run!

Down the other side came an old black gentleman who looked like something out of Central Casting as an Old Black Gentleman. He quite literally even had a handkerchief on his head and overalls with just one strap. He shuffled with what looked like arthritis.

The buildings were tall enough that neither party could see the other party coming.

My heart stopped. I thought, "Well, this is where the rubber meets the road, girl. You've marched for civil rights, you've tried to speak up when it mattered. If there's trouble, are you willing to put your body on the line?"

The two parties met up at the corner. The young men removed their caps and stood respectfully and said, "Morning, Mr. Johnson. Please say hey to Miz Johnson." And he allowed as how he surely would and asked after their families. They exchanged a few more pleasantries and then the boys put their caps back on and they all walked away and went on with their lives. By a miracle, no superhero help whatsoever was needed from an ignorant Northerner who felt she had made an ass of herself even if only in her own head.

And I remember quite clearly thinking, "Well, THERE'S a scene that will end up on the cutting room floor in a Hollywood movie about the South." I didn't know the phrase yet, but it would never "fit the narrative." We didn't have "narratives" yet, just reality.

It was a life-altering moment that blew away a lifetime of assumptions.

About a decade later on a brief January getaway to Barbados with the same best friend, we were walking back to our hotel from a restaurant, and we may even have imbibed sufficient Bajan rum such that we were not exactly in fighting form. We noticed three young Black men across the street and saw them purposely cross over to meet up with us. Uh-oh. (Just ask Jesse Jackson if that seemed a little worrisome…)

They stood a non-threatening distance away and said in that delightful sing-song island accent: "Our island and our jobs depend on tourism. We just wanted to thank you for coming and hope you enjoy yourselves." We all shook hands, they crossed the street again, and my friend and I wondered aloud if we had dreamed the whole thing.

SCIENCE GRRRLL

October 16, 2015

I know that I absolutely should not drink coffee after mid-afternoon. It will interfere mightily with my sleep. But I love coffee, and also sometimes my energy flags in "mid-afternoon," which I believe is an imprecise time frame that stretches until 8:00 p.m. Similarly, I believe that "late, late middle age" covers the years from the mid-50s to 5 years from wherever I'm currently at.

My problem has always been that I'm not convinced that the Coffee Rule has been adequately proven. Being devoted to Science as I am, I think the experiment needs to be run many more times.

If you doubt my massive Science credentials, I hasten to inform you that in addition to high school Biology, I fulfilled my college science requirement by taking a course called Physical Geography. Sadly, the course was given at 8:00 a.m. I often signed up for courses at that hour. Because, once you slept through them, you could sail guilt-free through the rest of the day. You didn't need to waste valuable psychic energy dithering about whether or not you were going to continue to play poker in the student union or actually go to the class. The class was over. Shut up and deal! Jacks or better to open and 4's and 9's are wild.

It also represented another kind of experiment. Can you skip many many weeks of Physical Geography lectures and labs and still get a decent grade? Define "decent." I received my first-ever

"C" in Physical Geography and that was a gift. It was mostly due to the fact that an engineering-major suitor at the time worked for dozens of hours on a comprehensive map which represented a large portion of my grade. He/We got an "A" on it which raised my grade from an impending "F" to that coveted "C."

It would be hard to get more Science-y than that. In essence, if you want to get all technical and judgmental, I cheated. Which would position me nicely for a career as a global warming scientist, where the dog is constantly eating their irreproducible data and they need to "hide the decline." But only for 18 years so far. Babies were born and graduated high school, and STILL no evidence of warming. That's some settled science going on right there, Boy Howdy!

But back to my current ongoing science experiment: Never mind the fact that of the 2,384 times I have run the Coffee Rule Experiment thus far, I have always had trouble sleeping if I drink coffee after 4:00 p.m. What about the 2,385th time? The results could change. That's how important I think Science is. And the sacrifices I am willing to make in its Holy Name.

The Coffee Experiment is not my only scientific endeavor. Far from it. I also have learned that if I don't make a grocery list, the odds of my coming home with what I set out to purchase go down substantially. But, again, given the many exhausting seconds it takes to make a list, has its utility been adequately proven? And who doesn't enjoy returning to the store – looking for a different checkout lady as far as possible from the last one – to get THE most important ingredient for the casserole you are making? The one item you went to the store to get in the first place.

So what if I didn't remember Cream of Chicken Soup? We are now the proud owners of five pounds of pistachios AND a bag of Double-Stuf Oreos. Though neither item is going to work in that casserole, they were on sale. What could go wrong with expired Oreos anyway?

I have heard it said of very smart people: "He has forgotten more things than I'll ever know." If forgetting things is the Gold Standard of intelligence, I must have at one time been right up there with Mr. Hawking. (My book proposal: A Brief History of Time-Wasting.)

Which brings us to the Second Martini Experiment. After one delicious Cantaloupe Martini, a specialty of my favorite local Italian restaurant, I can follow a conversation, possibly contribute the occasional witty or erudite remark, and even compute a proper tip. After two martinis, I like to take a short nap in my entree (ravioli is most comfortable) and I am quite certain that $50.00 is 20% of $80.00. The happy waitress has alerted other servers via her Facebook Page that it will be worth it to come in on their day off to be my server. "Bring her lots of butter and a free second martini! You'll thank me."

It's hard for me to comprehend that at one time in New York City, the "3 martini lunch" was quite common for bidnessmen. Yikes! And they allegedly went back to work afterwards!

You just never know. Some day that Second Martini Experiment may work out just fine for me if I keep running it. It's Science. Barring a merciful coma, I'm going to need at least two martinis a day to get through the next fifteen months.

CHARADES

October 23, 2015

On my recent road trip to and from Arizona to Minnesota, I had to pass through a checkpoint in New Mexico. Several uniformed Border Patrol men and vehicles were clustered around. A few relaxed drug-sniffing dogs were hanging out as well. Everybody hates someone who holds up the line, especially when it's 110 degrees and you have to roll down your window. So, with uncharacteristic restraint, I didn't ask, "What do you do if you find someone who is not here legally?"

Because the answer, of course, is "Absolutely nothing. We're not allowed to." The only way an illegal could maybe possibly get deported would be if he refused to bake a cake for a gay wedding.

Not that it will ever come up. I had my car CD player blaring mariachi music, and when asked by the agent if I was a citizen said, "Si, senor." The only thing I could have done to look more suspicious was hand him Ahmed's "clock," or scarier yet, bite a Pop-Tart into the shape of a gun. Nobody asked for any kind of proof, or, God forbid, an I.D. My word was good enough. Now, granted, I look about as Hispanic as Paris Hilton, but the guy just waved me on through with a slight smile.

An elaborate and very expensive charade. An old Jewish guy we know who had had the misfortune of living in the Former Soviet Union told us bitterly, "We pretended to work and they pretended to pay us."

In this case, just the pay is real. I imagine that some union would raise hell if every single Border Patrol Agent were fired or laid off. So better to pay them and then just not give them anything to do. I do not blame the agents. Everyone knows where the policy is coming from.

The Democrats will soon get nine to eleven million more voters, distributed nicely to change every red state to blue for all time. The Chamber of Commerce will get the cheap labor they salivate for. The rich liberals will get nannies and housekeepers from Guatemala and El Salvador and yard guys from Mexico. And the open-borders crowd will get to congratulate themselves on how open-minded they are, how morally superior to us crude "nativists." At least until some thug shoots their daughter.

Everybody gets a trophy!! It's win-win for everyone except the taxpayers, unskilled workers who have to compete, and school districts in border states like mine. Oh, and the nostalgic Constitutionalists who fondly remember a country of both freedom and laws. Plus a few random daughters who will get unenforced laws named after them as a parting gift.

Here's another expensive scam: green signs. Somebody – not you or me of course, but somebody – got a contract to put up many signs that say "Don't drink and drive" on the Interstate. Lord even knows what each one cost.

"Don't drink and drive" is a lovely sentiment, but who, exactly, is that aimed at? Shouldn't those signs be inside bars instead of on the Interstate? If you're not drinking, it's pointless. And if you're already drunk, what are the chances that you are going to see that sign, smack your forehead, and say, "Oh, man, I have been drinking and now I'm driving, which, despite 50 years of relentless propaganda, I never realized was wrong until this very minute when I saw that expensive sign. What can I do? Maybe go fast to get off the highway sooner."

This is roughly as effective as a green sign near the pregnancy tests at Walmart that says, "Don't have irresponsible, unprotected sex." That ship, my friends, has sailed.

There are other signs that say, "Dust Storms May Exist" followed by "Use Extreme Caution." Apparently, just regular garden-variety caution is insufficient during dust storms. Which may or may not exist, like Bigfoot or the insurance plan you could keep if you liked it.

Soon we may need color-coded Degrees of Caution. Level 1 – Puce – continue texting while drinking coffee. Level 3 – Lavender – grip wheel tightly in the "ten and two" position, swivel head back and forth continuously. Level 5 – Magenta – pull over and get in fetal position; wait for government to come help.

Important Reminder: Always Use Extremely Extreme Caution in the fetal position. Pray that while in the fetal position you are not found by chatty, wine-swilling Planned Parenthood spokes-ghoul who may loot your organs. Remember, simply being alive is no deterrent to organ salvage and sales.

(Planned Non-Parenthood assures us they aren't doing any more what they never were doing and people only thought they were doing from the "edited" videos of conversations that never happened. Yup. It's all good because they aren't doing what they weren't. Just so we're clear.)

TIPTOEING (PAST THE GRAVEYARD OF FORMERLY FREE SPEECH

October 30, 2015

Way back in my misguided leftist days in San Francisco, I knew two families with wildly-varying child-raising philosophies. One couple had a lively little boy who ran barefoot in damp, chilly, meeting halls that exhibited the same standards of hygiene as many radicals did personally. He ate hot dogs, chips and candy, some picked up off dirty floors. He was bright and energetic and never sick.

Another couple had a little girl who was a hothouse flower. She was fed organic baby food and kept far far from other ragamuffin children and any adult with even a sniffle. As anyone who knows anything about immunity would guess, she was sick most of the time.

My mother was a clean freak of the first order, but her sister (of blessed memory) bordered on the insane on the subject. She boiled her children's Monopoly pieces and tried to put the board in the oven to sterilize it. (That didn't work out.) Her kids (my cousins) couldn't play in a sandbox. Every letter we ever got from them mentioned one or more of the kids being down with the flu.

When I was a young mother, I tried to chart a kind of middle course. I had learned by that time from observing others' experiences, that it was a yuge mistake to tiptoe around when the baby was napping, whispering to everyone, "Shhhh...the baby's asleep." Consequently, our son learned to sleep through piledrivers on the street outside his bedroom and knock-down/drag-out (or more accurately, drag queen) fights coming from the apartment above us. That flat was occupied by two large, high-strung gay men. I gathered from the shrieking, this was not a monogamous couple, yet at least one person was not on board with that, or as the saying goes, "comfortable" with it. They may have been gay, but they still fought like men. It often sounded like a saloon fight choreographed by John Wayne.

A couple weeks ago, I opined on the horrendous damage to our language and our freedom by the cossetted SJWs and Pajama Boys who are allowed to have speakers disinvited, CEOs fired, and entire subjects closed because they feel "unsafe." Everyone around them is forced to respond to "microaggressions," a meaningless synonym for "nothing."

The damage to our Republic by caving to this utter nonsense is hard to calculate. But what about the damage to the shrinking little violets themselves? I am totally serious. What happens to those around whom people are forced to tiptoe?

I know for a fact that if you always tiptoe around an infant, she will never sleep through a night and will startle at the drop of a pin. She will be anxious and fearful.

Life, my dear friends and readers, is very, very tough. Nobody escapes unscathed. I am not talking here about the extraordinary courage necessary to storm the beaches of Normandy, go house to house in Fallujah, or raise a flag at Iwo Jima. I am talking about ordinary life. If you can't stand to have a speaker on campus with whom you disagree – for a speech you aren't even going to attend! – you are going to fold like a cheap card table at the first sign of any real trouble. How are you going to survive a layoff? Where will you find the strength to take chemo? How are you going to deal with the sudden death of a spouse, the incomparable pain of the loss of a child, the very real possibility of some day ending up with a serious disability?

We pamper our children at their peril. It's tantamount to denying them vaccinations to shield them from all adversity, challenges, and differences of opinion.

Not even to mention the peril to a legal system wherein the standard for a tort has traditionally been something that would be offensive to someone "not unusually sensitive" when EVERYONE is "unusually sensitive" and must be catered to.

RED STATE BLUE STATE

November 6, 2015

Since the advent of color television, election-night coverage has featured two separate colors for states on the electoral map. But the color scheme had not solidified until the 2000 election. In fact, Wikipedia says that as late as 1980, the networks were still using Blue for Republicans such that David Brinkley opined that the 44-state landslide for Reagan made the map "resemble a suburban swimming pool."

In 2000 the current Red and Blue scheme caught hold and stuck. It is easy to imagine that there must have been quite the heated discussions at the networks. Because at the time there was still widespread anti-communist sentiment. Certainly the Democrats didn't want to be saddled with being called Reds, despite Warren Beatty's rather gauzy, sentimental portrait of life in the Soviet Union in a movie by that name.

Well, now that the Democrats have let the cat out of the cellophane bag on their real socialist agenda, can't we call the states that go for them Red States again? They are dang proud of it. Their pale codger candidates are vying for who can shred the most Amendments, who can punish the successful the harshest, who can promise the most freebies, grab the most guns, hate the military and LEOs the fiercest while releasing the most criminals. Oh, and if you like your deodorant, better stock up on it. But mostly Hill and Bern are all about who can recycle the most thoroughly-discredited political ideas.

Openly advocating socialism – except as a quaint aberration like

Debs – is new. Also recent in our history is the obsession with what divides us rather than what unites us as Americans.

Kids when I grew up were proud to live in a "melting pot." *E pluribus Unum* and all that. From many, one. A simple saying acknowledging "the many," while not implying the slightest denigration of the many. It spoke of a synthesis, a unity, something greater than the sum of its parts. As a child, I imagined that pot filled not with food, which doesn't actually melt, but with various metal bars melting into one alloy, stronger, more resilient and better than any single metal.

Hiss! Boo! Racist Heresy! Almost as bad as "All lives matter!" And lo, "one" became the "loneliest number" and Diversity-Worship was born.

The melting pot, so yesterday, meant that we were all just one undifferentiated mush, doncha know. I don't know a single person who thought of himself that way, do you? New metaphors arose to explain the wonders of Diversity. Here are just two I heard constantly:

See, we're not just a pot where we all blend into one. We're a Beautiful Quilt, with dozens and dozens of different squares of cloth, vibrant and unique. Uh-huh.

This from people who have never MADE a flippin' quilt. I have. A bunch of squares sewn together ISN'T a quilt. Yet. It's just one layer. A quilt has a single piece of backing, a warm inner layer, and many, many ties to hold all three layers in place and make it into a quilt. Your metaphor dies a-bornin'. Because the "backing" in this instance is the the Declaration, the Constitution, our history, our commonality and the ties are the dozens of cultural bonds, not the mostly-superficial differences so beloved of the grievance-mongers like the color or shape of our skin.

OK, epic fail on metaphor. Try again. Let's go with the ever-popular Salad Bowl. Instead of melted mush in a big pot, behold the beauty of a salad! It has many colorful vegetables and maybe some cranky onion rings, and in a fancy restaurant, maybe even some nuts and sprouts. Again, it's not really a salad yet. It's a bowl of wet vegetables. What makes it a "salad" is the base of some kind of greens, and then the all-important dressing, the thing that pulls it all together. Man, we're still stuck with that whole unifying thing again.

Besides, as the t-shirt says, "No good story ever began with 'So, I was eating a salad'..."

Since most Diversity Drones can't do anything else useful, it's hardly surprising that they can neither sew nor cook. The only math they can do is to religiously count how many black people, how many Hispanics, how many gays and transgenders, how many women are on board any enterprise (except the NBA, of course).

Naturally, some people are more diverse than others. Jews, East Indians, Asians (always all lumped together by these sensitive bean-counters, never mind profound differences between Japanese, Koreans, Vietnamese, Hmong, Chinese, and Filipinos), all straight white men, and Conservative women of any color don't count for spit. I have mentioned before that I was once called to see if I could perform at a Diversity Conference in Minneapolis that was being held on Yom Kippur, the holiest day of the Jewish year. They didn't even have the good grace to be embarrassed or apologetic.

What say we take back Blue and make the electoral map into another swimming pool? And begin the Long Slow March back to *e pluribus unum*.

ASK NOT

Ammo Grrrll remembers a different sort of Democrat this week in ASK NOT:

November 13, 2015

I grew up in a rock-ribbed Republican family. My mother's family hated FDR, who at the time was President for Life like Papa Doc in Haiti. Mama will go to her grave believing that their family was discriminated against by the local Democrats in the Dust Bowl in the Dirty '30s. At nearly 95, she still speaks bitterly of the grapefruit and oranges of mythic proportions that Democrat families received from some government agency which theirs did not. It may sound trivial to you, but it made a huge impression on a poor little girl who got a single orange for Christmas. I think if the local Democratic party wanted to win her over, they should present her with a dozen enormous grapefruits from Texas and a note saying, "Sorry we're late. Our bad. Didn't mean to skip your house there in Astoria, SD in 1934."

So I was hardly inclined to be impressed by the Kennedys. But I was a teenage girl, not vision-impaired, and had never seen anything quite like this clan. I thought JFK was "really neat." Sure, he was "old," like all adults. But he was handsome and witty and articulate; he was a war hero. Like our family, his had lost the oldest son to the War. His wife was unlike any woman I had ever laid eyes on, some sort of sophisticated creature from another planet with her big sunglasses and lovely clothes. She sure as heck didn't shop at Penney's or wear the dowdy cotton housedresses my grandmas and aunties wore on the farm.

And the whole sprawling athletic family spoke with that Massachusetts accent that sounded so exotic next to our soporific speech pattern that could be called Minnesota Nasal, perfected by Walter Mondale, bless his heart. Not to throw stones in a glass house: I can't stand to hear myself on tape to this day.

Yes, yes, yes, we've all been treated to the exposure of every minute facet of JFK's life and proclivities since then. Unlike you and me, evidently he was an imperfect person. Several of the remnants of that family seem to be batcrap crazy. Who knows? Maybe it has a deleterious effect on children when their fathers are murdered by either a Communist creep or a Palestinian loser with the same first and last name. But, my, what a figure Jack Kennedy cut at that time and place. Especially to a small-town 14-year-old girl.

Our family listened to President Kennedy's magnificent 1961 inaugural speech, remembered now mostly for "Ask not what your country can do for you; but for what you can do for your country." It made me so proud to be an American. My parents did not vote for him, but even they thought it was a good speech. And he never attacked his fellow Americans once for belonging to the other party. Or pranced about crowing to half the electorate, "You lose! I won!" Imagine!

Let me quote just a few paragraphs, conflating some prose. The original is available for you to Google any time. Take a look. You will weep at how far this country's leadership has departed from the ideals he expressed then.

He asserts "… that the rights of man come not from the generosity of the state but from the hand of God." {oh-em-gee, did a DEMOCRAT say THAT??? With the God thing and all? Catholic clinger!}

"Let every nation know, whether it wishes us well or ill, that we shall pay any price, bear any burden, meet any hardship, support any friend, oppose any foe, to assure the survival and the success of liberty." {Exactly like Obama, except that he will support any foe and oppose any friend while trying to lose every conflict slowly enough so that it's the next guy's problem.}

"To those nations who would make themselves our adversary…we dare not tempt them with weakness." {What? No such thing as an adversary. Just friends we haven't caved to yet. Weakness is Putin being on "the wrong side of history." Tremble, Putin, tremble.}

And, of course, the big finish with "Ask not what your country can do for you." Seriously?

Can you imagine any Democrat who hoped to be elected saying any of that today? Why, today it's ALL about what your country (read: "taxpayers") can do for you! Been a thoroughly-unrepentant criminal? Not a problem. We're issuing an edict that no potential employer can even ASK! Hightailed it away from your platoon to join up with the enemy? Not a problem. Welcome home! Invite your parents to the White House! Enter the country illegally? Not a problem! Have a baby and some food stamps! Got a penis but feeling kind of girlish today? Aw, go ahead, shower with the girls! Only bigots could possibly oppose that.

Work any of this address into a Ted Cruz stump speech and watch the Democrat media hacks lose their minds. Today, the leftists in the Democratic Party would consider JFK a heartless Tea Party "loon," a "Taliban-wing" religious nut; a saber-rattling, anti-government zealot, probably belonging on a domestic terrorist watch list for dissing "the state."

And just by the by, not ONE "I" statement in the whole address. No, not one.

THINGS THAT MAKE YOU GO "WHAT??..."

November 20, 2015

So, I'm drivin' along on my last big road trip between Arizona and Minnesota and I come to some merged lanes, rapidly-descending speed limits, and the usual ten guys leaning on the shovel while two or three work on a very small section of road with many miles conveniently blocked off in either direction.

And then I see the cautionary orange sign: "Kill a construction worker, it's a $10,000 fine AND you lose your license!!" WHAT?? Miscreants beware! Do they really need that second threat?

Would anyone think: "If it were JUST the $10,000, that might be worth it, but the license thing…that would give me pause"? People tell me that all caps feels like yelling. So, here's me yelling: ARE YOU KIDDING? That's IT? You've just KILLED A HUMAN BEING!!

Is there any other instance in which a person could take someone's life, fork over ten grand and just take public transportation for the rest of his life? Do tell. Because I actually have $10,000 and "I have a little list… and they never will be missed." Just kidding, of course. Oh those rascally Gilbert and Sullivan fellas. That song makes me feel "unsafe," "marginalized," "uncomfortable," "invalidated," "triggered" and many other negative emotions as soon as I think some more up. Even the word "trigger" is particularly triggering.

So is this what we've come to in America? You kill a construction worker and pay a fine, but you defend your wife who has had the temerity to joke around about hypothetical Hallowe'en costumes that could possibly offend a humorless, mentally defective Stalinist, and you have to throw yourself on your sword to preserve your job? Whatever pathetic courses are required to earn a degree in college today should include The Groveling Apology 101. Followed by Advanced Weeping Resignation Letters of Shame 202.

I have burned several bridges in my life, some stupidly. But it is unthinkable to me to have to go before a slavering mob of thugs and cretins and confess my sins in order to keep a job. Which seldom even works, by the way. You ever see chickens when they fight? One gets a little blood on her and the others go into a frenzy and peck her to death. No lie.

So, no, I would not apologize for expressing my opinion. I would sooner beg by the freeway entrance. I always took the rather cavalier attitude, "Hey, I was lookin' for a job when I found THIS one…" Eventually, I became self-employed.

Eagerly I await the day when an attacked administrator – of any gender – finds his or her metaphorical testicles have descended at last. I recommend a huge sound system that can drown out the ensuing meltdown from the spittle-flecked crowd.

The accused should also be wearing a sombrero and a Redskins t-shirt, to prove that the snowflakes can gaze upon these items and still survive, and say the following:

"Fasten your seatbelts, you blithering idiots, grab your Play-Doh and plush toys, cuz it's gonna be a bumpy ride. You useless teachers who spawned these Baby Brown Shirts are all fired. Your jobs will be posted tomorrow. From this day forward, only people who believe in academic freedom, free speech, free press and actual diversity of ideas will be hired. Sue me. I will drag out any litigation until the end of time. It will make the Mark Steyn/Michael 'Hockey Stick' Mann case, now in its fifth year, look like a New York minute.

"Anyone who was yelling anti-white obscenities – which, by the way, absolutely is racist – at people trying to study in the library is hereby expelled.

"Call your Mommies to come get you, using your beloved cellphones, the technology for which you hysterical ninnies of various colors and genders have culturally appropriated from smart white men, including, but not limited to the Israelis you slander and boycott. Without white men, you'd be talking through two Dixie cups and a string.

"I can't do anything about a random yahoo in a pickup truck who is not a student here, yelling the n-word if, indeed, this incident even happened. If he were a student, he would be gone, too. Should you shoot out his tires, it wouldn't upset me, but if you are as bad at shooting as you are at scholarship, you would probably only hit innocent bystanders.

"Exams will be held on the posted schedule. Anyone not showing up for them will get an F.

"Sane adults do NOT call the Police when their feelings are hurt. The cops have better things to do. Oh, and by the way, ALL lives do matter. And Islamic terrorist murder is way way way worse than a poop stain in the shower, whether it's in the shape of a swastika, a hammer and sickle or Justin Bieber. Did you somehow miss the Electric Company song, 'Three of these things are like the others, but one of these things isn't the same?' Note to self: we will have to include it in remedial courses. Those of you still enrolled: Go study for your exams. You are a monumental embarrassment to me, this school and all its alumni. Dismissed."

MARGINALIZED! (THANK GOD!)

November 27, 2015

Marginalized is a silly, imprecise word thrown around a lot by the Perpetually Furious Grievance crowd without the slightest notion of its definition, let alone any documentation that deliberate "marginalization" exists. It sounds good, in that it sounds like something bad to be, something to whine about, and something one can blame others for.

(Parenthetically, I can live with being marginalized; I just hope I am never "margarine-alized." I'm strictly a devotee of butter. But back to our topic...)

From what I see in the tabloids week after week, being in the center of the action rather than off on the margins is more a recipe for personal disaster than a cause for celebration. You couldn't pay me enough to be a Kardashian. Plus, even counting hundreds of "celebrities" I am only dimly aware of from the wretched magazines at the hair salon, the "A-List" people comprise a vanishingly-small portion of the population.

The amount of energy it takes to maintain one's "A-List" status must be exhausting. I figure I'm on around the "N-List" (Nerds & Nobodies), with each passing year slipping another letter down the alphabet.

Even the most celebrated will eventually be shunted to the margins. Marquee athletes are forced to retire; movie "stars" get replaced by younger ones. One day you're a music idol; the next day, not only is your music no longer played, the entire genre is gone. Formerly-powerful and influential VIPs find that people will no longer return their calls.

Outside of parenting, I have rarely had any power, for good or ill, over any other person's life. (Brief conversation with 6 year old Ammo Kid after two days in first grade: "It's almost supper time, honey. Please clean up these toys." "You're not the boss of me." "Who told you that, son? Oh my, how mistaken you are. That is exactly what I am. Now clean up these toys.")

But, apart from that, no boss of anyone. I have never been management material; heck, I was barely employee material. For a few years in the '80s, a mere 30 years ago, I had quite a bit of input over who got to be in an annual women's comedy showcase at a popular Twin Cities theatre. (Answer: pretty much any woman with 10 minutes of material and a pulse.) And I hated even that amount of power. There were several people who should have been let go that I retained for years because I didn't have the heart to fire anyone.

So, okay, little to no power: check. Despite my massive Pinkish-Beige Skin Privilege.

Here are all the cool unmarginalized things I was not: cheerleader, Homecoming Queen, varsity athlete, any kind of athlete, President of anything, Student Council Member, or rich.

Here are a few of the decidedly uncool things I was: Daydreamer, Bookworm, A-Student, Championship Debater, average-looking grrrll on my best day. A very handsome actor friend admitted once that "being good-looking is like having an E-

Z Pass through Life." It is true for everyone, but especially for women. Bill Maher once joked (paraphrasing from memory): "I went to a party with my girlfriend and this gorgeous thing walked by. My girlfriend said, 'Would you leave me for her?' and I said, 'I'd kill you for her.'!"

Haha. Glad he's not my boyfriend, and I know it's a joke, but every average-looking girl knows there's a ring of truth to it and it hurts. But you get over it and develop other assets such as a sense of humor, kindness, cooking skills, did I mention sense of humor?

Since Thanksgiving was yesterday, let me enumerate just a few of the blessings that have been mine, living even as I do way off to the margins: two loving parents; good health; a wicked-smart, adoring husband; wonderful, loyal, funny friends; a beautiful son; the chance to travel all over this great land for three decades plying a successful comedic trade; and, of course, this awesome country and its heady freedom and unlimited opportunity.

And there is not one screaming, hysterical protester of any color, any real or pretend gender, who would be prevented from having any of those blessings. Not one. Healthy habits, good friends, a loving partner, children, an enjoyable career – all within anyone's grasp.

To all the embarrassing whiners manufacturing the most petty grievances, I say: Learn what's really important. What's the over/under on how many BLM supporters knew who "Calhoun" was before they were told to be enraged about a building named after him? And now that you know, it affects your life how, again?

Grow up; shut up; and get a life. Your massive, gratuitous rage will only raise your blood pressure and shorten that life. If you think your life will be improved away from the racist, rape-culture-y hellholes of Harvard Law or Dartmouth or Princeton, for the love of God, feel free to give up your spot to the next poor soul. Hey, maybe even to the applicant with 400 more SAT points than you whose place you took because of the color of your skin. Maybe she would have cured cancer instead of pretending to worry about John C. Calhoun.

FIT TO BE TIED

December 4, 2015

Every week I plan to work out with weights on three alternating days. Most weeks I actually do it once or twice. I want to stay strong enough to rack the slide on my Sig Sauer P227 .45. Not to mention carry my go-bag filled with my three favorite guns and several boxes of ammo in various calibers. My weight workout usually takes about 30-35 minutes, so you can readily see how a person such as myself, retired, an indifferent housekeeper, responsible for a once-weekly column that may run to several paragraphs, could have difficulty finding that crazy kind of leisure time in any given day.

Most days the intention to work out goes the same way as my intention to learn Spanish. The spirit is willing but the flesh is weak. And getting weaker by the minute. Especially in the triceps area.

It is also ever thus with my Bucket List resolution to reread *Moby Dick*, without skipping the boring technical parts about the ship or the stupid whale this time. Mr. Ammo Grrrll assures me that it is a great book and I will like it better than I did in 11th grade. Though long ago he did put the ki-bosh on my suggestion that we name our first-born child Queequeg. How cool would that be to have a name with not one, but two, "q's"?

In Arizona, each day dawns with a fresh new opportunity to work out. There is virtually no chance that you cannot get to the gym because of bad weather. Well, in my case, that's particularly true because I work out in my living room. A borderline agoraphobic, I kind of invented "sheltering in place." The house is sometimes messy, but I can almost always navigate from room to room.

But assuming that I DID go to a gym, there's still no hope of being rescued by inclement weather. Back in Minnesota you could always count on freezing drizzle or a blizzard with white-out conditions to provide a perfectly acceptable excuse. In Arizona, hoping for a haboob is not a realistic option. But when they do come, they are spectacular and usually make the national news. In time-lapse photography.

(And another great name: "I'd like to introduce our son, little Haboob. You remember his older sister, Queequeg. And their baby sister, Orange, whom we named after reading about Gwyneth Paltrow's child, Apple. Some day we hope to compare Apple and Orange just to see if it can be done.")

I do better on the aerobic part of my workout. As I've mentioned before, in the cool months (both of them), my walking partner is our neighbor, The Paranoid Texan.

But for many months a year I walk alone INDOORS when the temperature hovers around 200 Degrees in the shade. I may have that slightly wrong. Doesn't water boil at 212 Degrees Fahrenheit? (They don't call me ScienceGrrrll for nothing…) OK, from mid-April to late October, it's a few degrees off the boil, but not many. The wussie-pants snowbirds and Canadians flee in terror. Even our permanent residents take off for higher elevations.

During those months, I like to walk at Walmart. Seven times around the inside perimeter is about three miles. Not only is it temperature-controlled, but there are drinking fountains, multiple bathrooms for when you've overdone the drinking fountains, and doughnuts to keep your spirits up. There are also many inspiring examples of what one could look like if one does not work out. Many. Perhaps I serve as a cautionary example to someone else.

Our little Geezer Enclave in the Dusty Little Village (DLV) also has a very nice swimming pool. I do swim sometimes anticipating the glad day when the 100-Meter Flail becomes a sport in the Olympics. Reserve my spot on the winners' platform! Many of my fellow Geezer-Americans prefer to just stand in the pool and chat, blocking all the lanes for swimming laps. Which reminds me again it's time to tackle *Moby Dick*.

ON STRIKE!

December 11, 2015

It has come to my attention that all four bloggers on Power Line are pale males. Surely something must be wrong with that. I hope at least one of them is thinking of becoming transgendered. Sadly, the adorable names Chelsea and Caitlyn are already taken. Whereas the PL Boys are fine male specimens all, as females, I'm picturing them more as Berthas, Hildas or Mabels (not that these aren't also fine names).

Every time I try to open a new jar of peanut butter I am reminded that I am a grrrll, and that, because of my puny upper body strength, pathetically-low testosterone, plus the whole historical oppression deal, I am therefore entitled to Special Victim Status. It is not enough that you let me play in your reindeer games every Friday. More must be done. Always more. With the perpetually aggrieved, nothing is ever enough.

Inspired by the student ninnies at various asylums of higher learning, here are my demands:

1. Immediate upgrade to VIP Status. Enough already with the pop-ups. In fact, upgrade ALL women commenters! We have suffered enough from various uninvited pop-ups.

2. Acknowledgment of your white male privilege deal. Blah, blah, blah badly-written imperialist something. Blah, blah, blah racist, sexist, homophobic whatever gibberish. No need to list specific sins. You're all married guys, right? Vague amorphous guilt is

sufficient. All husbands learn early that they must have done SOMETHING they should be feeling bad about.

3. A groveling apology for not leaving my column in the first position for a minimum of four hours every Friday. Heck, sometimes it's not even there for four minutes. What's up with that? I wake up in Arizona at 6 a.m. and find that I'm already in the 3rd slot. Do you think another Muslim terrorist attack is more important than a humor column? As if! It's because I'm a grrrll, isn't it? Admit it.

4. No more soccer, Paul. Why? Because I don't like it. And I'm from an historically-oppressed gender. Game over, side out, as you folks say. And some teams have offensive names that make me feel unsafe. Arsenal – are you kidding? Talk about a triggering word! Manchester United? Doesn't being "united" imply that one's multiculti differences are discounted? Might as well call it Manchester Hateful.

5. Inclusiveness is so important. Creating a safe space for the delicate ladies. Let's incorporate a recipe exchange, camo fashion tips, and possibly a long list of distressing medical symptoms for notorious hypochondriacs to check daily. Not that I know any.

6. All of you smartasses, but Steve in particular, must check with me in advance to make sure you don't post something funnier than I have prepared for Friday. Commenters are not exempt. Avoid one-upping the columnist with more humorous comments. It can be hurtful and cause a columnist to call the police as we are urged to do by college administrators whose obvious insanity doesn't mean they don't sometimes receive perfectly good ideas through their dental fillings, tinfoil hats, or Son of Sam's dog.

7. Speaking of Steve's Week in Pictures, he frequently fails to include a sufficient number of attractive guys with guns as well as the hot ladies. He features far too many cisnormative semi-clad women which can cause deep and hurtful feelings of inadequacy, even when we are pretty sure we could outshoot the hotties. Don't make me dial 9-1-1 again. I'm beginning to suspect my local police department is not even taking me seriously. Especially when they put me on speakerphone and say, "You have GOT to hear this…"

8. All expenses paid trip to the next NRA Convention in Louisville in May. Also included on the free trip will be the winners of a contest to see which lucky three gun-friendly commenters can say the most flattering things about my work. Contestants, please include pictures. Of your favorite guns. Will write a subsequent 10-part series of NRA columns upon return. No? Okay, how about 2 commenters and 2 columns? Just me? Listen, guys, I need something FREE here. If not a Harvard education, how 'bout an NRA T-shirt?

9. Please respond to these demands within 24-48 hours. Or later, if you're busy. Though, be advised that since I don't fly, I will need to start driving to Louisville pretty soon.

(Seriously, dear readers, per efforts already underway from others, please join the NRA today, or upgrade or donate. It's very very important. And you get a great magazine. Though I'm a Sig Grrrll myself, the Kimber ads alone are worth it, many suitable for framing.)

ALTERNATIVES TO LEARNING

December 18, 2015

Year after year here in our Dusty Little Village (DLV), the education establishment puts an initiative on the ballot to increase property taxes for schools. For eight years and counting, it has failed. It will fail again.

Most of us Geezer-Americans have scant interest in donating even more to educate half of Mexico or to fund all the Diversity Drones and special programs whose gentle ministrations crank out the annual crop of psychotic ninnies infesting our colleges.

Year after year the local educators and some well-meaning parents cry about "class size" which they obviously believe is their strongest argument, though facts about class size are hard to find. Anyway, this does not impress us Baby Boomers because we rarely had fewer than 36-40 kids in a classroom. Our parents and grandparents went to one-room schoolhouses containing every grade, and had to do backbreaking farm chores before and after school. Yet we and they still managed to learn enough to earn a living for 40-50 years.

Have you ever seen those 8th grade tests of yore on the Internet? I can't pass 'em, that's for sure. At least not without refresher courses and studying up.

Let's look at just one special program we funded in Minnesota.

Back in the day, when we were raising foster kids, one of them was sent to what the educational system called the Alternative Learning Center. In the bureaucracy's desire to expand the number of dues-paying members and, tangentially, give second (fine), third (okay), and twenty-fifth (way too many) chances to lazy, disruptive, incorrigible students, this program was born. It should have been called The Alternative to Learning Center.

It demanded close to nothing from the students placed there. Basically, it required showing up. And many the student could not manage that. The other students called the ALC "A**holes' Last Chance." Kids can be brutally insensitive. (Call the cops!) Also accurate.

Anyway, the ALC contained a few pregnant girls plus plenty of "baby daddies" and other assorted miscreants. I honestly forget why our foster son was temporarily sent there. When you deal on a daily basis with drugs, gangs, and endless acting out, it's hard to keep track. But I do recall that he told me that in his ALC class they did not do homework, did not take tests, or learn anything. Plus, the "teacher" – who was "really cool, man" – was smoking weed with his little charges. Well, then. What could be cooler than that?

In a Herculean collaboration between genuinely heroic, sainted teachers, helpful fellow student tutors (all white and racist in their DNA according to Obama, despite his own polluted DNA), and, okay, his foster parents, our Black/Hispanic foster son did actually receive a high school diploma.

He was functionally illiterate in both his native Spanish and English, knew absolutely nothing about Civics, Science or History, and could neither add nor subtract, to say nothing of mastering algebra. Yet he graduated. Wrap your mind around that. What that made us realize was just how hard the 50 percent or more of students who FAIL to graduate at inner city high schools have to be trying in order to avoid meeting the most pathetic standards.

But that is YOUR fault, dear readers. Definitely not the individual lazy, hostile student. Nor the indifferent, negligent or distracted parent(s). But you, the taxpayers of the districts. Most particularly white people. And you will pay dearly when the "disparate impact" lawsuits are settled. There is an embarrassing, apparently-intractable gap between the performance of white and Asian students and students "of color." Those lawsuits charge not that the students and their parents have failed, but that the "system" has failed the students. But, of course.

Education is supposed to be a spoon-fed automatic delivery system in which the most uncooperative student has the absolute right to have the same outcome as that Chinese violinist who spends four hours a night practicing. (Or the Jewish math whiz, the Vietnamese spelling champ, or the pale-faced Norwegian debater who all study from the time he/she gets home to the time he/she goes to bed.) All tests that measure either aptitude or achievement are racist on the face of them and unfair. Everyone is entitled to a free diploma and then free community "college" to pretend to learn what should have been learned in middle school.

The Dr. Ben Carsons, the Dr. Thomas Sowells, the Condi Rices and even motivated recent African immigrants are resented at least as much as white people because they give the lie to the notion that somehow the "system" is gamed for only white kids to achieve. These individuals and thousands of other high-achieving blacks and Hispanics prove that all they have to do is exert similar effort to achieve similar results. Good God, *that* will never do.

MERRY CHRISTMAS!

December 25, 2015

What we have learned from forty years of "Diversity" and "Multiculturalism" is not tolerance and respect for differences of either opinion or culture, if, indeed, that was ever the point.

What "multiculturalism" has wrought is an unseemly, undemocratic, thin-skinned prickliness and hair-trigger eagerness to take offense. Plus a relentless race for Gold in the Oppression Olympics. Outside of doctors who treat high blood-pressure, how has our society benefited from this orgy of overreaction to the slightest most unintentional "microaggression"? That such an idiotic word even exists is evidence of how far we have fallen as a culture.

We've gone from "Live and let live" and "Don't sweat the small stuff" to "React instantly to any real or imagined slight – litigate, legislate, regulate, or riot." What a joyless, lonely mob of prigs, babies, and bullies we have become!

Surely among the most trivial of microaggressions is when someone cheerfully wishes a Merry Christmas to someone of a different faith (or none at all). Reasonable people can disagree with me on this; feel free to get your own dang column. But this is my opinion:

We can't have Valentine's Day parties in school because Valentine was a saint. We shouldn't celebrate Columbus Day or Thanksgiving because it's insensitive to the Indians. Hallowe'en is offensive from several viewpoints, not even counting the fact that for some reason, women often take the opportunity to dress up like hookers. And, heaven forfend if a store clerk dares to wish us a Merry Christmas.

Are we seriously better off because there are no mangers in the public square – banned by an unholy alliance of killjoy atheists and hypersensitive non-Christians? So, you don't believe in God? How much more sophisticated you must be than I, a mere clinger who also has a gun! Or you are Muslim, or Hindu, or Jewish? Mazel tov. Me, too. How 'bout we shut up and avert our eyes from the offending tableau, or tell our children that "This represents a very important day in somebody else's belief system. The vast majority as it happens. We don't celebrate that, and are not required to because of this great country we live in, but many of our neighbors do enjoy these displays. It doesn't hurt us in the least, as you can plainly see!"

The very same people who loathe the notion of the American melting pot because it supposedly trivializes or erases our all-important tribal differences are nonetheless compelled to say "Happy Holidays" because they have been told that is so much more "inclusive." But it isn't. It is meaningless mush.

It does not make me feel "included" to be wished "Happy Holidays" when Hanukkah has been over for weeks. I lit my candles and ate my potato pancakes and doughnuts and had a grand time. Except for three unwanted pounds that are sticking around in a festive manner, that holiday is gone. Now the calendar has moved on and it's Christmas.

My best Christian friend always sends me lovely greeting cards for specific Jewish holidays – Hanukkah, Passover and Rosh

Hashanah – and I send her Christmas and Easter cards. She has to put some effort into it as such cards are not occupying much shelf space in our Dusty Little Village's emporia. We don't do "Happy Holidays." See, we TRULY acknowledge our cultural differences and respect them. We don't paper them over with generic twaddle.

How did it hurt me in any way when, as I left the office last week, my dentist's new receptionist wished me a "Merry Christmas"? I now had a couple of choices. 1) I could smile as graciously as one can with Novocain and say "Thank you, and same to you!" or, 2) I could sigh heavily and make a big, stinking issue out of it in front of everybody in the reception area. Which would force her to apologize abjectly. Cripes, in some quarters it might cost her her job! Social Justice Warriors just plain LOVE it when someone loses his or her job. "Cel-e-brate good times, c'mon!"

Of course, I could tell myself that it was a "teachable moment," a chance to explain that it isn't my holiday. But what is that, really, but a smug opportunity to lecture and embarrass a perfectly nice human being who wished me only joy? The Torah is quite adamant and repetitive about not humiliating others.

"Ah," say the complainers, "Don't you think it's offensive when everyone just assumes that you are a Christian?" No, I don't. I know who I am. And I am secure in that knowledge. Inadvertently glimpsing a manger or having a flyer for Easter Ham put in my grocery sack at Byerly's will not threaten my beliefs. Though it did make me laugh – out loud, even – because the whole bag was filled with matzo and many other Kosher for Passover items. That's what's called a "clue."

Today is Christmas. In the last month, many good-hearted strangers have expressed the wish to me that this day be a "Merry" one and I intend to make it so. I advise all my fellow Americans to do the same. I will also light my traditional Sabbath candles 18 minutes before sunset. That will be merry, too. A little more light and a lot less heat.

THE HOME STRETCH: JANUARY, FEBRUARY and MARCH 2016

The columns in this period, naturally, deal primarily (no pun intended. Really.) with the electoral primaries.

There is some minor excitement in the Republican primaries as all the smart people debate about which of the ludicrous number of contenders would stand any chance at all against the Inevitable Coronation of Queen Hillary. The smart money says it's a done deal. It will just be a matter of picking which Republican patsy will run a weak, crappy campaign and fold like a cheap card table in the face of any criticism about being mean to the Queen.

Former Secretary of State Ms. Albright informs us that there will be a "special place in Hell" for any woman who fails to vote her uterus. Later, it will turn out that that special place better be pretty capacious, but we don't know that yet. Ah, the beauty of hindsight!

A bizarre thing keeps happening on the campaign trail. This tall, billionaire, reality tv star with the hairdo whose sole purpose seems to be to annoy people, keeps failing to get knocked out. Everybody knows it will happen sooner or later, and if it doesn't, that the Republican Party will not recover for "generations". (Meanwhile, back on campus, it appears that there may not even BE more "generations" because young people are terrified of and disgusted by sex. Is there ANYTHING the Left can't ruin? But think for a moment what it takes to ruin an interest in sex.)

On a personal level, one minute I'm turning in a column on the Terrible, No Good, Very Bad War on Women represented by poor John Kasich trying to give a shout-out to the ladies who helped elect him by coming out of their "kitchens" (Gasp! He said women were in kitchens!) and working for his campaign. And a few days later, I got that terrible phone call at 6:30 am from my brother that Mama had died in her sleep. Nothing good can come of a 6:30 am phone call. It's never Publisher's Clearinghouse informing you that you have won the Sweepstakes, is it?

She was a lifelong, hardcore, rock-ribbed Republican and would have loved to vote for President Trump. Being a Republican and not a Democrat, she could not vote after death. No trunk full of only Republican ballots, including hers, was ever found in a car trunk in Douglas County. But, I like to think that if there was any Divine intervention involved in the 2016 election, that she helped persuade the Holy One, Blessed be He.

WEIGHING IN

January 1, 2016

It's January First and the official close of The Eating Season that opened on Hallowe'en. Some perfectly-reasonable people contend that The Season extends all the way to Super Bowl Sunday, if not Valentine's Day. In general, these people are not battling anorexia.

Mr. Ammo Grrrll just bought a fancy new digital scale, but I don't like it at all. I don't need an instrument so precise that it tells me that I am one-something-something POINT TWO. You can't screw around with a digital scale like you can with an old-fashioned scale, finding that sweet spot to stand on to shave off a couple of pounds as you weigh nekkid AFTER going to the bathroom, but BEFORE putting on your deodorant. They frown on that at the doctor's office. Evidently.

I should mention that my relationship with scales has not always been positive. And I don't even count the one I threw into the basement that time when it was obviously lying its fool head off. My girlfriend Angela gave me a birthday card once with two adorable little toddler girls in the bathroom, and the one standing on the scale says to her friend, "Look! I'm standing on Mama's crying machine." Ah, truer words…

In my experience, weighing leads inexorably to a Hot Fudge Sundae. How so, you ask?

Listen and learn. IF you think you weigh, say, 138, and it turns out you only weigh 136, you say, "Woohoo! I am doing so great! I DESERVE a Hot Fudge Sundae!" On the other hand, if you think you weigh 138, and, God forbid, you weigh 139.4, you say, "I have been on this diet for over three days and have failed to achieve my goal weight. Nothing works. I am an abject failure and will always be fat. I MIGHT AS WELL have a Hot Fudge Sundae."

See how I did that there? My advice: don't weigh. Unless you really want a Hot Fudge Sundae.

It would seem to be no accident that "gluttony" made the cut for the Seven Deadly Sins. What is fine as a rare treat or even in moderation seems to plague us when we go overboard. And yet the impulse to go overboard in every realm is ever with us.

Do NOT put a tray of Lemon Bars in front of me, go away for a period of time, and expect to find many on the tray when you return. I'm sorry; I'm weak. That will reduce me to trying to rearrange the remaining bars on the tray in such a way that it will make my gluttony less obvious, like some sort of pathetic culinary "comb-over" that hides a bald spot.

The Torah admonishes us to "not put a stumbling block in the path of a blind person," and a reader might say, "Well, that's a stupid rule – who would DO that?" Not so fast. We see it every day. The "friends" of the alcoholic who encourage their buddy to have just one little drink. The single guys who take their married buddy to a strip club when they know his wife hates it. The waiter who refills my chip basket in the Mexican restaurant even after Mr. Ammo Grrrll attempted to put them out of my reach before that unfortunate incident with my fork. The person who bakes

Lemon Bars for a Friday columnist and then leaves the room.

The Indians smoked tobacco ritually, as I understand it, as a rare communal event with the peace pipe and all. They never envisioned that this could turn into a three-pack-a-day habit for a sane person. The late, great Jerry Garcia, who apparently tried to pack a hundred years of hedonistic pleasure into just 50, was reputed to be a five-pack-a-day smoker. As a former smoker, who not infrequently lit the new cigarette from the dying embers of another, "chain"-style, I still only managed to go through three packs.

When I read about the mind-boggling sexual appetites of some people – 10,000 partners for this NBA star, a paltry 5,000 for that relative piker of an actor – nothing about that sounds fun or even interesting.

It could be one of those gender things, like finding The Three Stooges amusing. But to me, 10,000 different partners mostly sounds busy, dangerous, empty and sad. Ten THOUSAND? Seriously? The math alone is daunting. One a day for 30 years? 4 a week for 50 years? 10 a week for 20 years? The score-keeping is problematic as well. A notch on the bedpost would reduce your bed to splinters within weeks.

Without a spreadsheet (This is a family column. No obvious puns, kids. Tracy, Alasdair, Jay C, this means you), how would you even be certain you hadn't counted some lucky partner twice or, God forbid, skipped one?

But, 10,000 Lemon Bars – now, we're talkin'.

A very Happy New Year to the Power Line family of bloggers, commenters, and readers. Praying for a year of peace, prosperity, good health, laughter, and conservative victories. May all your personal resolutions for good be accomplished with relative ease. Especially the ones still standing by, say, January 3.

ARE YOU FROM THE RIGHT CLASS?

January 8, 2016

More than 8 years ago – what seems like a lifetime ago now – when Sarah Palin was chosen to fill the vice-presidential slot on the GOP ticket, I was astonished and appalled to discover how many snotty people had a visceral personal hatred of her, mostly irrespective of her politics. Including many many people who should have known better.

I was delighted by her speech at the convention. She was – hands down – the best speaker of the four candidates in 2008, including Mr. Creased-Pants Reader of Gibberish off the Teleprompter Himself. But she was a happy, beautiful, married woman, a breeder, a Christian who refused to kill her special needs baby, a strong supporter of Israel, a hunter and basketball player. She didn't even own the proper clothes to run for office. In short, she was not at all from the right clique, so she had to be destroyed. The vicious campaign to belittle and destroy her was like watching a nature show with a whole drooling pack of ugly hyenas stalking a defenseless gazelle. It made me sick.

Two core beliefs in America are that all honest work is noble and that we are all "middle-class." But what I took from the Palin experience – and its terrible aftermath of consequences for the country – was that there is an elite class of people who went to the right schools (hint: none are in Idaho), and married the right people (not part Native American fisherman, certainly!) and live in the right zip codes. They hold many of their fellow Americans in utter contempt. I looked at these people and paraphrasing a bit of Sally Field at the Oscars, realized, "You hate us; you really, really hate us." You probably can hardly tell that I'm still angry.

My therapy – when I can't get to the range – is humor. So, here's a little quiz to determine what rung you might occupy in the caste system. Are you a donor-class celebrity, a pathetic loser-person who pays taxes, works hard, is proud of your kids' military service, or someone Hillary's virtual husband (Future First Horndog) fancies, who Hillary has called "trailer trash"? (I mean no disrespect to any class except the donor-class celebrities, 99 percent of whom are not nearly as smart as they think they are. Every single commenter on Power Line is smarter than all but a handful of Congress critters and left-wing celebrities.)

We are painting with a broad brush here, as humor will. No animals were harmed in the making of this quiz, which also contains no gluten.

My name: a) Appears on clothing the "little" people buy. b) Is sewn into my underwear from college many, many years ago, or, c) Has been changed to protect the innocent.

My thighs: a) Do not touch. b) Would have been eyed hungrily by the Donner Party.

The last film I appeared in: a) I got top billing. b) Was in 8 mm of me, Harold, and our six kids at Disney World, or, c) Was around the bathtub.

My home: a) Is on a private island of underage slave girls, accessed by a private plane called The Lolita Express. It was visited by the pretend husband of a Presidential shoo-in. b) Is all on one level because of bad knees, or, c) Has to be staked down in strong winds.

To relax, I get into my: a) Hot tub which seats 18 comfortably. b) Old flannel nightie with a good mystery, or, c) Jack Daniels.

I think guns are: a) Icky, and should be banned like in Australia, except for those carried by my private bodyguards. b) A right bestowed upon me by our Founding Fathers, or, c) Necessary to provide dinner.

My dresses: a) Each cost more than a 3-bedroom home in 1955. b) Sometimes don't zip all the way up, or c) Cost less than arugula. Whatever that is.

My teeth are: a) Capped, b) Used to open child-proof caps, or c) Not as numerous as my tattoos.

My weight: a) Is lower than my body temperature. b) Fluctuates more than the stock market, or, c) Is appropriate for a 7'8" man.

Whenever I put on a couple of extra pounds, I: a) Jet off to the Golden Door Spa for two weeks. b) Go the the "Y" to work out for two hours, or, c) Have only one scoop of ice cream with my pie for two days.

My car is: a) In a temperature-controlled warehouse with more than 100 luxury vehicles. b) A sensible mid-size sedan. c) A truck.

I was educated at: a) Elite Ivy League schools. My applications and grades are buried with Jimmy Hoffa. b) State schools, or community college, or, c) My Dad's auto-body shop. Can YOU replace a transmission, PoliSci Boy?

PLAYING BY THE RULES

January 15, 2016

The propensity to make rules for others to follow – somehow lawmakers always manage to exempt themselves – is truly astonishing. We have recently witnessed another weepy backdoor attempt by the President to immiserate the lives of law-abiding gun-owners while leaving the "refugee" terrorists, the criminals, the insane, free to continue with theft and straw purchases. This site has dealt very well with the issue and I have nothing to add except I sure would like to get ahold of some of that half billion to "study" the problem some more.

So I will just try to do what I'm here for, which is to entertain.

Except for the relentless gun-grabbers, perhaps nowhere is the tendency to overregulate more vilely displayed than in Home Owners Associations. We had never lived in a gated community or anything but a rather hang-loose working-class neighborhood before we bought our Dream House in Arizona.

We were used to neighborhoods where some people had manicured lawns and others hung their laundry on a clothesline in the front yard; some people mowed when you could no longer find the smaller children, and others used tweezers to extract every single dandelion. When we moved into our suburban house – itself a yuge step up from our basement apartment on the East Side of St. Paul – the family of four teenage boys next door had a big net in the yard with which to practice soccer goals for three seasons, and hockey slapshots for the other. Bang, bang, bang, slap, slap, slap. We lived with it and they lived with the fact that we had a roaming outdoor tomcat who annoyed the heck out of their elderly, near-blind dog.

In our Dusty Little Village, we were forced to sign in blood that we would abide by the Phoenix Yellow Pages-sized set of rules governing our HOA before we were even allowed to buy our home. We didn't read the rules, of course. As with Obamacare, we were encouraged to sign on to them to "see what's in them." The last time the Jewish people signed on to something without reading it was The Torah, which turned out to contain several zany surprises. "No coveting OR shrimp? Really?"

The main problem with the HOA is the failure to have just a few common sense rules. We can't just say, "No laundry in front. Don't paint your house plaid," and be done with it. Oh, no. We must specify the only nine allowed colors. Plus the ONE color for the fences; the ONE type of chicken wire to prevent the rabbits from eating all the landscaping; the ONE caliber of bullets with which to shoot the rabbits.

Haha. I kid. HOA rules specify only nonviolent methods of dealing with rabbits, such as encouraging them to commit suicide by playing in an endless loop, the tape of Obama's speeches that he gave to the Queen, apparently as a gag gift. The Paranoid Texan Next Door planted allegedly poison bushes, but the rabbits ate them right down to the ground without discernible ill effects.

The other problem, of course, is that many people do NOT have any common sense and so everything must be spelled out. In my experience, left to their own devices, homeowners will amass many kinds of demented lawn statuary: the inevitable pink flamingos, bunnies with bonnets, lighted deer, bears, cows. I figure these are transplanted country folk, living in the big city who miss their rural environment.

Which would open up a whole new market of lawn statuary for city folk who move to the country and have nostalgia for an urban setting: little panhandlers with their handwritten cardboard lies; small mechanical flashers in their grubby raincoats; gangstas in brightly-colored backwards caps; and one lane into the driveway permanently blocked off with orange cones and a Merge sign.

My former yard man, Enrique, gifted me with a little burro pulling a wagon which sat in the front yard for a few weeks until we received a letter citing the chapter and verse in the regs that prohibited yard art in the front yard. Or at least Mexican yard art. We have noticed examples of frogs, bleached steer skulls, and at least one orange ceramic pig that somehow passed muster. Unfortunately, the letter arrived in June when we were back in Minnesota.

Burdened with an insanely anti-authoritarian nature, when I called the Paranoid Texan Next Door, I said: "This is freakin' America! I will fight for that burro till hell freezes over." And he asked me if I had ever heard the song, "I fought the law, and the law won"?

He then shared that he had waged a multiple-months battle to match the color of his fence to his house rather than the one approved color of Icky-Old-Snow Grey. And lost. As a postscript, he informed me that after all the geometrically-increasing fines they can levy, they can actually put a lien on your house. At which point, Mr. AG took the phone and urged the PT to "please move her ass into the back yard" while muttering something about how I still had much to learn about picking my battles.

Sometimes I sneak the burro back in front for a few hours. Because this is America. At this stage of my life, I can always plead dementia.

THE UGLY AMERICAN (REVISITED)

January 22, 2016

Being of late, late middle age, I am old enough to remember when a whole best-selling book was written talking about what crude, rude, fat, loud, insensitive slobs we Americans were when we traveled internationally. Why, we expected the countries we were visiting to speak some English!! *Quelle gauche!*

Then, we had an invasion of several tens of millions of illegal immigrants. And a few million legal ones. And suddenly, instead of ragging on insensitive GUESTS, it was the American HOST COUNTRY that was fat and insensitive, rude, and – it goes without saying – racist! Why? You couldn't guess it if you had just read *The Ugly American*, but it was, in part, for failing to speak the guests' language. No, really! We were supposed to provide ballots, directions, signs in Walmart, and instruction in schools in Spanish.

Whoa! Didn't see that comin', did you? Damned for wanting English spoken abroad and damned for wanting English to be spoken in our very own country. As the President's sweet spiritual adviser, Reverend Wright said, "God damn the United States of America!" as its citizens can clearly do nothing right. How odd that so many people are trying to flood in to such a terrible place. And nary a soul risking life and limb to get out. You want to leave? There's the door! Bye-bye, Clock Boy and Daddy. Enjoy the heck out of Qatar.

Now, correct me if I'm wrong here but, to the best of my knowledge, Americans in Europe never marched in angry parades carrying American flags. They never demanded that France or Switzerland or Spain not only let them overstay their visas, but give over half of them welfare benefits. They never insisted they all get drivers' licenses and be allowed to vote in French or German elections. They never swarmed around young women in a mob gropefest or worse. Americans just wanted someone to tell them how to get to the Eiffel Tower while they spent their hard-earned tourist dollars on over-priced coffee and dry pastries that couldn't hold a candle to a raised, glazed doughnut in any hometown bakery.

Why, if you are demanding to be a legal resident of America, do you think brandishing a Mexican flag, for example, is the way to convince people that you give a crap about this country except for the free goodies? Ethnic pride, you say? It's long been a mystery to me why ethnicity, gender, sexuality, or race has anything to do with "pride" anyway, even the St. Patrick's Day Parade which would include many of my relatives.

I am a short, roundish, pale, enthusiastically-heterosexual woman. (The Grrrll from Arizona is sort of the polar opposite of The Girl from Ipanema who was "tall and tan and lean." We do both "go walking," however.) Anyhow, I was born this way and am very happy, though I wouldn't protest if I were a few inches taller. But I can take no credit for any part of it. Why should I be "proud" of something which is a complete accident of birth? Moreover, like many Americans, I am a mutt – a mixture of six ethnicities. That's a heavy parade schedule and bloated flag budget. I think I'll skip the whole hyphenated-American thing. Old Glory is plenty flag for me.

I am proud of my long-ago puny academic achievements, my long-term marriage, our great son, my semi-secret recipe for Brisket and Made-From-Scratch-Including-Pitting Fresh Cherries

Cherry Pie. Those are things I accomplished or achieved. I am blessed to be an American and profoundly grateful.

I am neither proud nor ashamed of my skin tone and would gladly be a darker shade if I could look like Halle Berry or Salma Hayek. You can't convince me that I benefited from "White Skin Privilege" when virtually every single person I competed against in the first several decades of my life was the exact same color. However, I sure did benefit from having two wonderful parents who were actually married and still are after 71 years. My father served in the Navy, went to college on the G.I. Bill, worked all but three days a month in his store, and supported us. Nobody was a criminal or substance abuser. Those cultural choices are available to all.

I shall not hold my breath anxiously awaiting an updated version of *The Ugly American* called *The Demanding Immigrant* in which the foreigners – both invited and invading – are taken to task for insisting that Americans speak their language. That road – like so many – only goes one-way.

WHY I AM BOYCOTTING THE OSCARS

January 29, 2016

Oh, mercy me! I realize that by now this is not breaking news but, evidently, black people have not garnered any nominations this go-round in the Oscars. Disaster! Black Awards Matter! It certainly could not possibly be that no individual black actor was outstanding enough in a good enough film to merit such acclaim in 2015. Oh, no. It's a racist conspiracy. Has to be. Wait. Didn't Denzel and Halle both win in the same year? Oh, well. That was then; this is now. And it was 14 years ago, to be fair. And Halle is just about to wind up her over-the-top wailing speech any minute now.

To be taken seriously, I would like Will Smith and all other protesters to state in every category exactly which black actor should have replaced which white actor for the nomination. Make them go on the record. (To force college Admissions drones to motivate why an Asian with 1600 on her SATs should be rejected for a more favored race with 1000 on her SATs is too much to ask.)

Just, by the by, where are the nominations of short, roundish women of late, late middle age? For too long we – uh, I mean they – have been ignored in Hollywood.

And so, because of black actors being deliberately snubbed, and short, *zaftig*, elderly women being similarly disenfranchised, I am throwing my enormous influence behind the boycott of the Oscars. Miscreants beware. Ammo Grrrll is on the case.

Why? Well, first of all, I always take my marching orders from the dynamic anti-Semite Al Sharpton. Anyone who has played a leading role in a bogus anti-cop rape accusation AND involved in a murderous riot, plus is delinquent in his taxes, and THEN gets his own television show has got to have something going for him, right? Luckily the job description does not include the ability to read from a Teleprompter.

I have reasons aplenty for my participation in this boycott beyond just the obvious racism of Hollywood Democrat Bag Men (and Bag Ladies. Gwyneth to Obama: "You are so handsome, you should be President forever." Good grief. A grown woman! And she gets to vote.).

I am boycotting the Oscars because I find the whole spectacle of a bunch of spoiled, overpaid, political poseurs of any color giving themselves yet more accolades and awards repulsive in the extreme. The so-called "swag bags" worth six figures which they use to bribe presenters to appear could certainly be better used to help Joe Biden find the cure for cancer or buy Al Gore some nice parkas and stocking caps for his global warming appearances during the inevitable blizzards that dog him wherever he pontificates.

I am boycotting the Oscars because if I never hear the idiotic question, "Who are you wearing?" again, it will be too soon. But I suppose it is a more tactful question than "You aren't going out of the house dressed like that, are you?" I have scant interest in seeing the assorted body parts of Beautiful Women tumbling out of transparent gowns. I'm not opposed to it, you understand, and realize that many men enjoy it, but it just does nothing for me. Especially if they aren't even carrying an interesting weapon. The fashion statement most of these ladies seem to be making is, "Look! I have breasts!" Me, too, girls, and mine are real.

OK, full disclosure: I have been unintentionally boycotting the Oscars for decades. I hardly ever watch them and actually have no idea when the 2016 incarnation is on. It is rare that I have seen any – let alone all – of the nominated movies. Almost everyone inside the Dorothy Chandler Pavilion is a Democrat blowhard whose bleatings do not interest me whether uttered in person or through their film personae.

But I think it's morally imperative that we ALL boycott everything from or about anyone who doesn't look exactly like us. Sadly, I will have to get rid of my Larry Fitzgerald t-shirt, featuring as it does, a near-lifesize photo of a person who is not only a man, but a black man. Bye-bye to watching any NBA game when five black men are on the floor at the same time. Which is, let's face it, most of the time.

I can't watch Ellen or Sheldon on *Big Bang* because I am not gay. I must boycott any salsa band with no anglos in it. I will boycott *Elementary* because I am neither a man nor an Asian woman. How sad and silly and circumscribed my life will become, but it's important to never be exposed to anyone who is not exactly like me. In fact, why even bother to know anyone else when I can just gaze lovingly into the mirror?

And finally, it is obvious that the very word "boycott" is sexist. It should be "personcott." I should boycott boycotts until this grave verbal injustice is rectified.

ABOUT LAST MONDAY...

February 5, 2016

My candidate did not win in Iowa. Who was that, you ask breathlessly?

Donco Cruzabee, that's who. I want someone with Ted Cruz's brains and debating skills, with the youthful good looks and inspiring backstory of Marco Rubio, the genial warmth and personality of Mike Huckabee, and the cojones, minus the gratuitous rudeness, of Donald Trump.

As I read the many many postmortems and comments on Power Line and several other sites, here are some of my more or less random observations:

ONE. As astute and always-respectful commenter, Deborah Brown has said we are going to have to resign ourselves to an IMPERFECT candidate. There is no perfect candidate who can satisfy every voter, or even every conservative voter. There is no Donco Cruzabee, and if there were, someone would find out that in 3rd grade he pulled a girl's pigtails and the NYT would run a 72-pt headline, "Cruzabee Has History of Sexual Assault." That's because:

TWO. These elections turn on idiotic minutiae that are blown more out of proportion than the old Barbie Doll's measurements. In a nation with crushing debt, foreign policy disasters, a vanishing middle class, the shredding of the Constitution, do we really have the luxury of caring whether Mitt Romney teased someone when he was 14? Or that someone drank too much water during a debate or even, God forbid, forgot his third point? Hell, I forget what I was going to say sometimes mid-sentence. For that matter, going back a few years, what possible difference did it make that Adlai Stevenson had a hole in his shoe? Are we all daft? When polled, we all say we want the candidates to have a "vision," to tell us what they are going to do, and we all hate the negativity. But we don't. That's why the oppo researchers are going great guns right now to inform us that this guy's great-great-grandfather wrote a private letter in which was found a racist word, and that in 1972 that guy called up "Information" for numbers he could have looked up in the phone book.

THREE. What's up with all the name-calling, my fellow Americans? Good grief! How trippingly on the tongue come shouts of "RINO!" and "Establishment!" and "Brown Shirts!" and then the truly juvenile insults like "retard." Why not just go full "doody-head" and "poopy-pants"? Are we not grown-ups? I am going to severely paraphrase a wonderful 25-year-old joke told by terrific standup comic Emo Phillips. I hope he remembers that I once reviewed him for a Twin Cities newspaper and gave his comedy album a rave and doesn't mind that I now "quote" the gist of his joke from memory.

He tells a kind of shaggy dog tale about meeting a Little John-like character mid-way through crossing a bridge and a standoff ensues. The man announces, "I am a Christian," and he replies, "Yes! So am I." The man says, "I am a Protestant," and he replies, "Great! So am I!" The man says, "I am a Lutheran!" and he agrees, "So am I!" The man says, "I am from the Missouri Synod!" and he says, "Me, too!" He says, "I attend St. Stevens on Oak Street," and the man says, "Die, Heretic!"

We have all been toiling in the vineyards of left-wing cultural domination for a long time. My friends and colleagues on Power Line, particularly Scott and John, have been in the trenches in Minnesota, arguably "the belly of the beast," for a decade or two. It would be laughable, if it were not both erroneous and depressing, to see the vitriol hurled at them for being insufficiently able to grasp the charms of Trump or the "treachery" of Rubio. They certainly do not need me to defend them. But why, when we all here have so much in common and the stakes are so high, do we allow ourselves to say "Die, Heretic!" to someone who has a slightly different perspective?

I do not believe that much will change even with a Republican win in 2016, even with a veto-proof Congress. "Lucy" has pulled the football away from me for too many times to believe in miracles. And Government, in general is a sclerotic behemoth that cannot be moved. My core issues are border control, Second Amendment rights, First Amendment rights, and pro-Israel/anti-terrorism foreign policy.

Donald Trump looked very attractive to me on these issues. Nobody hates Political Correctness more than I do. But is childish rudeness the same as fighting PC speech? Is it yugely smart to make insinuations about a newswoman's period or to call a brave and brilliant conservative like Michelle Malkin (who, by the way, has to hire full-time bodyguards for her children so numerous are the death threats) "born stupid"?

Nevertheless, unlike some, I WILL vote for Trump if he is our standard-bearer. I will also vote for Cruz, Rubio, Carly, or even Christie. I will vote for almost anyone against Hillary or Bernie or, for that matter, Gun Grabber-in-Chief, Bloomberg. I initially preferred Rick Perry, but for whatever reasons, he faded fast. This is a long slog. And very very important. Let's try to keep it as convivial as we can. Except for you crapweasel, neocon, neonazi, RINO-loving, douchebag Heretics who support that other guy.

MORE BAD IDEAS (AND ONE GOOD ONE)

February 12, 2016

Hoo Boy, is the electorate in a cranky mood! Primary voters from both parties seem to be saying, "No! You Democrats will NOT tell me which protected grievance monger will be inevitable. And you Republicans will not choose which spineless patsy will be unable to criticize her and lay down and lose as planned. This may turn out to be a Smart Idea or a Bad Idea. It remains to be seen. So today I will offer up a non-political thought or two.

We all do dumb things. Most of them are small mistakes from which we can recover. I have referenced in the past, holding a blender pitcher with the bottom off under the faucet such that it formed a perfect funnel and soaked my shirt. On more than one occasion. Embarrassing, yes, even if nobody else is around. But hardly fatal.

On the other hand, there may come a time when you too are forced to ask yourself: "Was eating a bowl of something called 'Nuclear' Chili, and a piece of very rich Heath Bar Pie a good idea?" Even allowing the excuse of having recently consumed an adult beverage or two with the sophomoric name "Screaming Orgasm," this was a bad idea. Well, short on the "Orgasms" but they got the "Screaming" part right. Thanks to the delicate yet volatile nature of my organs that are collectively called The G.I. Tract.

And while we are on the subject of tracts, and moving along briskly from the previous tract, was it a good idea to make eye contact with the disheveled young man handing out religious brochures in downtown Minneapolis last fall? No, it was a bad idea. Mr. AG, a former Chicagoan, has spent many decades trying to teach me the proper demeanor for riding a subway or walking city streets.

Eyes forward, kind of out of focus; shoulders squared, very brisk pace if walking. Make NO EYE CONTACT, even if a wino throws up on your shoes!

These were hard lessons to absorb for a naturally gregarious, small-town person whose mother cannot leave a restaurant, sanctuary or shopping mall without greeting every single human being, including a few mannequins.

Thus did I smile and make that forbidden eye contact and waste nearly half an hour of my life trying not to appear either the dreaded Minnesota Un-Nice, or worse yet, Racist.

(Parenthetically, my general attitude toward panhandlers is pretty much the same as my attitude toward politicians: "Just don't lie to me." I have given money to a bleary-eyed but honest gentleman who said, "Could you possibly give me a dollar to buy a drink?" But, don't come at me with some bullcrap story about needing money to get your car which just broke down on your way to a job interview. Or money for baby formula. Because I do not care to be played for a sucker and to have you think you have fooled me.)

But back on topic: Was it a good idea to "window shop" last week in joyous celebration of the fact that all of my credit cards were cleared? No. Another bad idea. I bought several things, none of them windows. But who could resist a church-key style bottle opener, which is also a magnet, with the AZ Cardinals logo on it? Or the 300th set of colorful placemats? Or the salt shaker with the exotic pink "Himalayan" salt? All items which would qualify for the "Beyond" part of Bed, Bath, and Beyond.

Was it a good idea to start another diet the week before joining Mr. AG on a business trip in a restaurant-rich city? No. It was a dumb idea, doomed to immediate failure.

But, it worked out happily because we were celebrating the 50th anniversary of the day we met as teenagers.

There are so many ways to almost ensure a life of misery: substance abuse, engaging in criminal behavior, failing to prepare for any kind of work. But Mr. AG and I have come to believe that THE most important decision you will ever make is not what school you pick, or what career you prepare for, but what life partner you choose. Some people do at least get it right after a practice run or two. We were just plain lucky right out of the box. And that, my friends, turned out to be a very good idea.

A SPECIAL PLACE IN HELL

February 19, 2016

Madeleine Albright says that women who fail to vote for Hillary just because she shares the same array of lady bits as we possess are going to a special place in Hell, reserved just for us. Based on the exit polls in New Hampshire, it better be a spacious facility, in which case, just how "special" can it be? Will it be nearer the buffet line or what? Maddy, define "special."

I am shocked, shocked, to discover that Ms. Albright even believes in Hell. Despite her many accomplishments – memorably chasing down the hall in high heels after Yassir Arafat to beg him not to abandon the conference before he agreed to the newest Screw Israel Piece Proposal — she's just another bitter clinger. Who knew?

We are ordered by The Sisterhood of the Traveling Pants-Suit to forget the fact that Hillary is a vicious attack dog running interference for her horndog husband against his female victims. (We hear a lot about RINOs. Bill is trying desperately to become First HINO – Husband In Name Only.) She is also a pathological liar, an influence peddler, and an obscenely-paid "speaker" who isn't even funny. But, as long as she's got one of those organs that routinely engages in Monologues unbidden, she's supposed to have my vote sewed up. Vote With Your Vagina! Think I'll pass and vote with my brain instead.

Donald Trump got taken to the woodshed – like he cares! — for repeating the "p" word. How long before every letter of the alphabet is a code for a naughty word that's been voted off the island? And now we are bullied into voting for every person who owns a "p." Well, that's not quite right. Certainly not Sarah Palin or Mia Love or any woman who doesn't believe in the "choice" of ending her baby's life right up to the time labor pains are 3 minutes apart.

I don't plan on going to Hell, no matter how special the accommodations Madeleine has arranged. She apparently believes she has some influence with the Devil, so I guess she feels qualified to arrange a special place for us. Madeleine, while you are negotiating that special place in Hell, say "hey" from me to Yassir and Helen Thomas, if indeed they are not the same person. You never saw them together, did you – hmmm? — and they looked almost identical except Yassir was marginally cuter and less anti-Semitic.

And I will never – no, not ever – vote for candidates on the basis of the color or shape of their skin or any other tribal marker, including being Jewish. The very idea is anathema to me. It is not "time" for a woman or a gay person or a transgendered Olympic athlete or a wise Latina, just BECAUSE they are one of those things. It is waaaay past time for honest, patriotic, qualified, Constitution-upholding candidates who are "brave, courageous and bold" and I don't care if ALL or NONE are from a grievance-monger category.

I do believe that one thing this primary season portends is that that tribal crap is so over outside of the outdoor asylums that educate our young. And even among the young, primary voters are flocking to a wacky elderly white guy. And also Bernie Sanders. The Very Special, Fabulous, Historic, Inevitable, Woman Candidate has all the traction of Bambi on ice, no matter how many campaign reboots she announces. She calls it sexism. I call it about time.

And finally, about the urgent need for women to "help" women, just because they are women: give it a rest, Madeleine. You were confirmed 99-0 by the heavily-male Senate nearly 20 years ago. Since then, there has been a Black woman Secretary of State, and then Hillary. No wonder you feel the need to lecture young women. Someone who is, say, 35 or younger, has never known a time when women couldn't be anything they put their minds to – doctor, lawyer, astronaut, general, business executive, news anchor. It's over. We won. And winners shouldn't whine.

THE FRACTURED FAMILY OF MAN

February 26, 2016

When I was in college, back in the quaint days when young men and women lived in separate residence halls, and not a single professor of Divisive Studies called for "muscle" to remove a student journalist from a public gathering, I bought a coffee-table book at a used bookstore.

The title of this book was *The Family of Man* and it was a beautiful picture book that demonstrated in photograph after photograph, our commonality and shared humanity. For example, there might be a picture of an American father bending down to correct some behavior of his small son, and on the opposite page there might be an African tribesman and his little boy with the exact same expressions on their faces.

There might be a picture of a beautiful Mexican couple clearly in love right next to a picture of an elderly Russian couple holding hands and adoring each other. "See?" each pairing seemed to say, "We are all just people, just part of the great human family. We laugh; we cry; we love; we fight; we make new babies; we grow old; we die."

When we were parenting a couple of foster sons in the early '90s, my Black/Hispanic son favored an expensive and colorful line of clothing with the motto "Love sees no color." He wrote an essay in his ESL class for Mother's Day in which he said, "My mother loves me as though she had held me in her arms on the day I was born." Boo! Hiss! Obviously, a white-privileged woman cannot love a Black orphan from Honduras.

It absolutely breaks my heart to realize how far our society has descended from the sentiment that "love sees no color". For the current arbiters of cultural norms assert that we have no common humanity. We are in a perpetual war of "each against all" except for the favored few in our own little tribe.

Today, we are supposed to see ONLY color, though those constructs are mostly lies. Bobby Jindal is a darker "color" than Halle Berry, but only one will be considered by the former head of the Justice Department, Eric Holder, to be a member of what he termed "my people." Ah, Blind Justice! We should have renamed his fiefdom The Department of Just Us.

Next most important, apparently, is our genitalia, both God-given and manufactured, and then, with whom we choose to share access to same. Far from embracing our common humanity, the impetus now is to drive us into as many tiny competing tribes as possible.

Are you Jewish? Well, good on ya, but are you a Jewish woman? Then many synagogues will organize your own Women's Seder apart from your Jewish brethren. I never have, even once, even when I was a loopy Democrat, attended. I had nothing to celebrate with women that I couldn't celebrate with my fellow Jewish men. I doubt that is now separate enough for the amoeba-like splitters. Coming soon to an SJW synagogue near you: The Gay Black Spanish-Speaking, Transgendered Differently-Abled Women's Seder! Enjoy. Both of you.

Tell me honestly, my friends: when you were marching for civil rights, equal housing, integration, did any of you believe there could come a day when saying "All lives matter" would get you booed and possibly beaten?

When you went out for tacos or Satay or General Tso's Chicken in 1985, say, did you envision a future time when you would be berated for "cultural appropriation" for patronizing the ethnic eatery down the block? Groveling apologies and reeducation camps clearly in order.

I'm afraid I do despair of ever returning to the days of The Family of Man, setting aside, of course, the outrageous word "Man." Just as I despair of returning to the days of good jobs, interest on my savings of 4%, stable marriages and raising children within the two-parent family. If you have any ideas on how to begin this process, please feel free to share.

I also believe that these things are much more important than which flawed, ego-driven, duplicitous politician wins in the November shell game. In 1964, all the smart people said that voting for Goldwater would ensnare us in a war which LBJ called a war "Asian boys should fight for themselves." I was too young to vote, but I worked for Goldwater and sure enough, we got horribly involved in Vietnam! So, Vietnam was all my fault and I apologize.

Well, now I'm off to culturally appropriate some Thai food. As offensive as that is to Oberlin students, the hard-working proprietor at Thai Dressing always seems downright happy to see me. What does he know? He probably never even took Thai Studies.

#WAR ON WOMEN--KITCHEN EDITION

March 4, 2016

Here is a surefire path to the Presidency: first, be no lighter than beige or tan. Hide every single detail of your murky past. Forever. Have no living relatives. Then, vote "Present" about a hundred times so that you can never be tainted with having an opinion. Spout gibberish in a pleasant manner until anyone with half a brain wants to stick a fork in her eye if she hears "Hope" or "Change" one more time in her life.

When asked – but I kid, he was NEVER asked! – what you are hoping FOR or what you intend to CHANGE, either suggest that your inquisitor hates "the other" because of his funny name or look off into the distance, chin raised, in an imperial way. Later, someone will put a glow-y halo around your head. This, of course, assumes that you are a Democrat.

If you are a Republican, your past will be subjected to what Rush has referred to as an "anal probe"; your garbage will be sifted, and every single word you say will be misquoted, wrenched from context, and thrown into your face. If you say nothing offensive yourself, you will be forced to say whether you agree with what the next guy, Todd Akin, for example, said.

Poor Kasich. He tried to tell a true anecdote, expressing gratitude toward women, about how he got elected to the state legislature in the '70s and he mentioned "women" and "kitchen" in the same sentence. Hater! Sexist pig!

So, this is what we've come to, now. The aptly-named Twitter came alive with the squawking outrage of a weasel-infested henhouse. And some really smart people are still wondering why Trump is ascendant?

I am no fan of John Kasich. I would vote for him against Hillary or Bernie, but then, I would vote for Harold Stassen (even dead), Chuck Norris, or Caitlyn against them.

But as a woman, I once again felt embarrassed for my gender and also felt sorry for Kasich whose only sin was telling the truth. Let us get the full Quote of Hate right: "How did I get elected to the legislature? I didn't have anybody for me. We just got an army of people and many women who left their kitchens to go out and go door to door and put up yard signs for me…It was an army of women that really helped me get elected to the state senate."

In the middle there, near the ellipsis, he also pointed out that that was then, this is now, and that now there are no more volunteers because EVERYBODY is out working, nobody is at home. He does not say or even imply that this is a bad thing. It's just what IS now.

In Jewish Temples, what is often called a Ladies' Aid group in churches is called The Sisterhood. Many years ago, our dynamic woman rabbi, feminist *par excellence*, gave a stirring paean to the Sisterhood which she called "The backbone of the Temple." These were the ladies who volunteered for everything from organizing fund-raising to teaching Sunday School, to baking pastries and cookies for the Friday night reception after the service. And guess what? Not too long after that, with that generation of ladies getting older, passing away, there were no younger ones to replace them. Basically, Sisterhood was no more.

Why? Because, just as Kasich said, everybody was now out working for pay. Nobody was in the kitchen except maybe Lupe, the Guatemalan nanny. Do not think for a moment that this does not affect every organization that has traditionally relied on an "army" of volunteer women.

Nor should you think that it does not do a massive injustice to disrespect those amazing women – including my mother and probably yours – who kept a house and raised several kids and also did all those volunteer jobs, both through organizations and through basic, human kindness. A death in the family? Casseroles and cakes would appear. A disabling accident? Ladies would arrange to take your kids to Little League, shop for your groceries, clean your house. For as long as it took.

If you think for a minute that these were less important tasks than what women do today – which, granted, are sometimes those things PLUS a job – then you think wrong. Kasich meant no offense; he gave no offense. Not to any sane person who was not looking for a reason to be offended; he spoke the truth. And in today's political climate, Truth is as unwelcome as that weasel in the henhouse.

A PASSING

POSTED ON **MARCH 11, 2016** BY **SCOTT JOHNSON** IN ANNOUNCEMENTS

THOUGHTS FROM THE AMMO LINE

We are sad to note the passing of Ammo Grrrl's mother this week, Ammo Grrrll is taking the week off. She asks that her readers and fans keep her in their thoughts and prayers. I asked if she would let us remember her mother by name. She responded:

We were blessed to have her for 94 years and 50 weeks. She would have been 95 on March 24. She died peacefully in her sleep after a day of shopping and setting up a lunch date with friends.

My mother's name was Dorothy Terry Baumbach, born in 1921, raised in Astoria, South Dakota, along with John Hinderaker's father's family, married to James Baumbach for 71 years, resident of Alexandria, Minnesota, from 1952 to the morning of March 9, 2016.

She was a pip, Scott, and hilariously funny. And a lifelong, hardcore Republican. We will miss her vote in November. Maybe, Chicago style, her death will be no impediment to her voting.

There is a hole in my world that will never be filled.

NANNY STATE NONSENSE

March 18, 2016

To channel the late and much-maligned Senator Joe McCarthy, "I hold in my hand, a special mailing from Xcel Energy, the spelling-challenged Minnesota utility company formerly known as Northern States Power, informing me of what an electricity-guzzling wastrel I am."

For it would seem that I have used 8% more energy than my neighbors! There is a colorful bar graph with Green (but, of course) representing the Good Efficient Neighbors, Grey for All Neighbors, and a long Blue Line of Shame representing ME, the Bad Grrrll, up an unconscionable 8%.

Why they should not be *delighted* that I am using so much of their product remains a mystery, virtually unique among purveyors of products. I await a similar letter from Ben and Jerry informing me that I have bought 8% more Cherry Garcia and Chubby Hubby Ice Cream than my most lactose-intolerant neighbors and asking me to please try to use less.

I am old enough to remember when NSP's little jingle went, "Electricity is penny cheap, from NSP to YOU!!" I guess in ridiculous Minnesota winters, with utility bills hovering around $300 a month at least, that slogan was laid to rest. That's a LOT of pennies. 30,000 of them if I can still do math. *(Scott: please check the math. I was a Sociology major...)*

Let us also set aside for a moment the bullying, intrusive nature of the whole enterprise, possibly plunging the more unhinged miscreants into a shame spiral at a minimum. Suicide at worst. Not everyone has my default attitude to authority which can be summed up in two words, the last of which is "you."

They do have helpful suggestions for conserving energy on the back of the letter. Great ideas like "unplug electronics and other devices." Yes, you read that right. Not just turn them off, shut down your 'puter, but actually unplug your television, DVR, game consoles and computers. Every dang night. They further suggest that if you forget to unplug all your stuff, you should try leaving this letter near your door. Yeah, that's gonna happen. Doing this every night – presumably resetting your clocks every morning – 12:00-12:00-12:00 –can save "up to" (weasel phrase) FIFTY DOLLARS A YEAR!!

It makes me so furious to be hectored like this, that it makes me want to turn ON my blender and my mixer and a hair dryer, if I owned one, and run them all night. (In Arizona, your hair dries on your way from the shower to the closet to select an outfit.)

If I want to squander a dollar a week, I will. I worked hard for many decades and I have no intention of unplugging and replugging 365 days in a row in order to save enough for one decent dinner out. (Truth to tell, in our DLV, it is nearly impossible to spend that on a dinner for two, unless you order drinks, appetizers, three entrees and dessert. And coffee.)

Which brings us to my final point: what in the name of all that's Holy did this LETTER cost to send out? The research, the graphics, the ink, the murder of the trees, the human labor, the horses slaughtered for the glue for the envelopes?

Finally, in a nod to the "Everyone Gets a Trophy" philosophy that defines Minnesota, the letter tells me that "In 2015 you used 13% less energy than in 2014." Woo-hoo! Then back off, nosy eco-freaks.

Actually, the credit for that reduction belongs to our son. Because, of course, we don't even live there.

Our Minnesota house is now occupied by our son except when business or elder care calls one or both of us back from Arizona. I happen to know that he sets the thermostat to about 65 in the winter, so all those lauded neighbors that are allegedly more energy-efficient than he is are the ones who go away for the winter and set their thermostats just high enough to keep the pipes from freezing. If you eliminate the snowbirds, I bet he wins walkin' away. My heart swells with pride.

P.S. To all the dear commenters who sent condolences last week, please know that they sustain me still. I have printed them out, put them in a special file, and will go to that well when I need to be lifted up. I have also shared them with my father and siblings. Anyone who thinks that those kinds of brief, heartfelt sentiments do not mean much to the recipients are mistaken. Thank you one and all.

MAN O'WAR

March 25, 2016

Many years ago, I went to Hawaii with my teenage son and his friend. For the friend, it was his first time in an ocean. We were all swimming and laughing and having a grand time, when suddenly his friend screamed in agony. He had been stung by a Portuguese Man O' War. Supposedly, it is one of the worst pains on earth that you will survive.

One of the beach bums rushed up and told my son to "Quick, bra, go pee on the sting."

I don't know whether this would have worked or not because, for some reason, the kid declined the treatment. But it got me thinking: "HOW did this idea originate?"

Did some poor wretch think, "Boy, my leg hurts like a son-of-a-gun, I wonder if it would feel any worse if someone peed on it?"

Speaking of terrible pain, I have heretofore not really weighed in on the Presidential contest except to say that I will vote against Hillary or Bernie no matter who is nominated on the Republican side. That is still true. I voted for McCain and Romney, too, and am not sorry. However imperfect they were, they were light-years better than what we got.

All comedians have a higher than normal need to be loved and I have been reluctant to attract the kind of vitriol and name-calling that has become an unfortunate new wrinkle on this site. I want everyone to look forward to my little Friday posts and not hate me for being beautiful. No, wait, that's a cosmetic ad. There is a vanishingly small chance of that. I don't want people to hate me for picking a different candidate from the one they are enamored with.

It would be hard to define a retired comedian of late, late middle age, roadkill on the Information Highway, swearing in front of a Windows 8 computer in a Dusty Little Village in Arizona as part of the "Establishment." But stranger invective has been hurled. So let me share my honest, sorrowful misgivings about this contest.

I am not biting my lip as I tell you this, but "I feel your pain." We have been stung mightily by the last 8 years, not by a Man O' War, heaven forbid with his Nobel Peace Prize and all, but by a Pouty-Pants of Fundamental Transformation. Who, in my opinion, is a vicious anti-Semite and anti-white racist to boot. And we have also seen the Republicans betray us again and again, not closing the border, not making government smaller, not reversing Obamacare, not doing a single thing they were elected to do. It is damn depressing.

So, initially, I thought Trump, in all his bombast and ego, in all his willful ignorance, was a breath of fresh air. And then he attacked John McCain's war record as a "loser"; he made a sophomoric reference to Megyn Kelly's period; he said American soldiers would commit war crimes for him; he says he will be "neutral" on Israel; he channeled Code Pink in attacking W over Iraq; he called Michelle Malkin "born stupid," and he is even backpedaling from his biggest selling point for me, closing the border.

And I wonder: is he the political equivalent of peeing on the sting? Do we hurt so bad that we will accept any remedy? Lord knows, he has assured us he has the impressive equipment to pee on us. And if there's anything I look for in a President, it's a distinguished member. How well I remember the history lesson in which George Washington took time from crossing the Delaware to send tracings of his fingers to a snotty reporter who had called them "stubby." Maybe that was someone else. History, like math, is hard.

On the other hand, we have a choice between voting for Trump who MIGHT close the border, who MIGHT be pro-Second Amendment, and Kasich who has already announced that there's not a snowball's chance in hell that he will do anything but grant amnesty to everybody in the first 100 days. And the gun-grabbing, open-borders Democrats. Chelsea has just promised her Mommy will give all illegals free medical care. Y'all come, hear?

And Mr. Cruz? I have already voted early for him here in Arizona. But I am not thrilled that a fellow Senator – even one as repulsive as Lindsey Graham – has said Cruz could be killed on the floor of the Senate and, if the perp were tried in the Senate, he would not be convicted. Good grief! Is that just because he's not a go-along to get-along guy who is trying to upset their shell game? Or is it something more fundamental about his personality that will bode ill for the general election?

So, correct me if I'm wrong, my friends, but it looks to me like the survivors who haven't been voted off the island include: a crooked, lying harridan who may soon be living in a new gated community, i.e., prison; a wacky, elderly commie who thinks we should manufacture just one brand of deodorant; a liberal loose cannon with a fluffy, orange comb-over; and a wicked-smart but weird, conservative guy nobody likes who reminds my friend John Hinderaker of Richard Nixon!

I've been reading lately that sitting is really bad for us. So I think I'll lie down. Wake me when it's over.

THE COLUMN TURNS TWO

April 1, 2016

Well, friends, be careful of hitting "Send" in an impulsive manner (always good advice), lest you become an inadvertent columnist having to think up a new topic every dang six days. Now that is nothing compared to the Power Line Boys, who have to think up topics or react to breaking news several times A DAY. Plus, take a ton of crap from the blogosphere for their efforts.

Which puts me in mind of a quote from the late, great Phil Woods, who was an outstanding jazz saxophone player. One night he was playing in a club and a snotty patron approached him and said, "Hey, man, all you do is imitate Charlie Parker." At which point, he handed his instrument to the guy and said, "Here. YOU imitate Charlie Parker for awhile."

Everything is harder than it looks. Writing a clever two-sentence "gotcha" criticism of something someone else has written is not the same as writing and researching the thousands of topics that the Power Line Boys have written. For a couple of decades. While holding down big-deal full-time jobs. And raising families. A little slack, if not appreciation for the effort, couldn't hoit. As angry as you think you are, these guys are not your enemy, I promise.

As you may remember from last year's anniversary column, in March of 2014, after standing in line several hours a day waiting for ammo with a diverse assemblage of shooters, some certifiable but fun, I thought it might provide grist for a column. I was almost always the only woman in line, and soon was called

Ammo Grrrll. I wrote a tentative opening inquiry to my friend, Scott, hit "Send" and a few moments later saw it appear in "print." What appears on the Internet, stays on the Internet. Forever. So now even my husband calls me Ammo Grrrll.

A year ago, we had a cast of dozens who wanted to challenge Hillary to prevent Obama's third term. At least half a dozen would have been great as either President or Vice President. I would have bet the ranch that the GOP (elite and Tea Party) would have gathered the contenders into a nice resort in a pleasant location and said the following:

"Look. We need to win one for The Gipper, and The Republic if it is to survive. We already start out with virtually all the mainstream media against us, a fact which is supposedly worth at least 15%. This is a war. Soldiers do not shoot at their comrades. You must all pledge to say nothing negative about any of your opponents that can be used as fodder for ads in the general election. You may tout your own records, your own visions, but you must show some discipline in refraining from attacks on other candidates. Save your fire for the real enemy. Moreover, anyone who violates this level of decorum will be banned from further debates. Calling people liars and worse will not be tolerated."

And so it went exactly as planned. And rainbows and unicorns were the order of the day.

Haha. April Fool! It could not possibly have gone worse if all the campaigns had been run by Hillary agents. Some conspiracy nuts claim that they were. Had I bet the proverbial ranch that things would go smoothly, I would be homeless now.

Further, we have an utterly fractured and fractious group of center-right voters who are hardening into enraged enemy camps. We have the "Anybody But Trump" crowd, the "If Trump Doesn't Get the Nomination, I will Freak Out" Crowd; the "I Will Stay Home" crowd, and the "Let's Blow up the GOP Altogether and Form Another Party" crowd. Meanwhile, the lying sociopath and influence-peddler cruises to her coronation, cackling all the way. Bill is taking applications for new interns.

Well done, GOP!! But there is more to Life than elections.

In my personal life, of course, I have just lost the beloved woman who gave me life, who was one of my best friends whom I spoke to every day. I mention this only for perspective, not for further condolences which you have already given in open-hearted abundance.

On the other hand, the sun is shining; it is 90 degrees in Arizona; my fat little baby hummingbirds are outgrowing their adorable, tiny nest. I have a loving family, a circle of supportive friends, a beautiful son and wonderful husband, a nice home, several supermarkets full of foods that the monarchs of Europe and robber barons of America could only have dreamed of, and excellent health. I will not be made miserable by investing too much emotion in this every-four-year spasm. I suggest you all count your blessings, have a stiff drink or go for a long stroll, and relax.

And thanks for reading my column.

AFTERWORD

And thus, ends Year Two of the Ammo Grrrll columns on Power Line. I feel pretty good about this Volume. Every writer struggles to find his or her "voice". I thank the Power Line boys, especially Editor, Scott Johnson, for allowing me to be me. I do not write like a lawyer or academic. And yet they let me make my contribution, week after week. I hope that this volume was even sharper, clearer, and funnier than the first book, Ammo Grrrll Hits the Target. Please order that book if you missed it to compare. You readers will be the judge of which is best.

Please stay with me for Volume 3 "Ammo Grrrll Returns Fire" when things really heat up after the name-calling by Hillary, a mistake that I believe cost her the election. Neener neener. And Praise the Lord!

My husband, novelist Max Cossack, is still peddling his first novel, Khaybar, Minnesota, on Amazon and by the time this volume sees the light of day, may have his second novel in play. He won't even tell ME the title, so just go to Amazon and search for Max Cossack.

I expect to have Volume 3 out by Valentine's Day, 2019. And Volume 4, "Ammo Grrrll Is Home on the Range" out by the 5th anniversary of the column at the end of March. For however long I continue at Power Line, I will release that year's column compilation in a timely fashion soon after the anniversary column in March, since I will then be caught up.

See you on Power Line. Be well. Be happy. Joy is like Kryptonite to the Perpetually Enraged Leftists. And Joy combined with Humor really frosts their cupcakes. You owe it to the fight for civilization to laugh and be happy. If I have contributed in any small way to that, I am grateful.
Susan Vass – Ammo Grrrll – December, 2018

www.ingramcontent.com/pod-product-compliance
Lightning Source LLC
Chambersburg PA
CBHW020411080526
44584CB00014B/1280